How To Manage Your Parents

by Copey Pulitzer

Illustrations by Nan Parati

Illustrations Copyright © 1992 by Nan Parati

Cover Artwork Copyright ©1992 by Sidney C. Pulitzer, Jr.

Manufactured in the United States of America

Library of Congress Cataloging-in-Publication Data:
Pulitzer, Copey
HOW TO MANAGE YOUR PARENTS
Library of Congress Catalog Card Number: 92-90914

ISBN# 0-9633496-0-0

My great appreciation goes to all the people I was able to get to read and re-read draft(s) of this book. A extra thanks to: Clifford, Mike, Albie, Sarah, Cheri, Dr. Usdin, Monte, Don, Mom and Dad. Also, a special thanks for the use of the poem on page 112, as it is an "Excerpt from <u>Gates of Repentance</u> is Copyright © 1979 by Central Conference of American Rabbis and Union of Liberal and Progressive Synagogues (Canada). Used by permission."

Published by Copey Pulitzer

This book is dedicated to my sister
and all older brothers and sisters
who pave an easier way
for us younger kids.

Table Of Contents   page:

Author's Note:

Dear Reader:

HOW TO MANAGE YOUR PARENTS is written to help you deal with your parents so EVERYONE WINS. This is accomplished through three steps. The first is a combination of evaluating what your relationship is with your parents, understanding your parents, and building communication with your parents. The second step is enhancing and sharpening your negotiating skills, and the last step is exploring the multitude of techniques, tools and tricks that are so incredibly useful to managing parents.

HOW TO MANAGE YOUR PARENTS is written in a very honest and frank way. When I wish to express my very personal or sometimes rather sarcastic thoughts, *the print will change as you see it now.* **Please do NOT be offended by any of my jokes, sarcasm, or name-calling. They are NOT intended to be hurtful or malicious, but are only extreme exaggerations written for FUN.**

I truly hope you find the following pages interesting, entertaining, and most importantly, helpful. Consistently maintaining a good relationship with our parents may be difficult, but is achievable. It takes hard work, understanding, patience *and sometimes an electric cattle prod.* I wish you the best of luck!

Sincerely,

Copey Pulitzer

Chapter 1: Our Relationship With Our Parents

Once upon a time there were identical twin brothers. They were the same in every way except that one was always happy and the other was always depressed and upset. Some psychiatrists heard of these twins and decided to try an experiment. The brother that was always happy was put into a plain room with piles and piles of horse manure. (This room probably smelled worse than my mom's cooking.) The other brother was put into a beautifully decorated room with all sorts of fun toys and games.

After leaving the twins to get acquainted with their rooms for awhile, the psychiatrists decided to check on each of them. When they walked into the beautifully decorated room, they could not believe their eyes. The boy that was always depressed and upset was sitting in the corner of the room crying uncontrollably. When asked why he was crying and not playing with any of the toys, he told them that he was afraid to play with them since he might not understand how they worked, would not like them, might break them, etc. He expressed every possible reason why he would not even try to play with the toys.

The doctors were amazed and decided to visit his brother. When they walked into his room, to their even greater surprise, they saw the boy having a wonderful time! He was running around the room frantically digging deep holes with the horse turds flying everywhere! All the while, he was laughing and screaming in joy. When they asked him what he was doing, his response

was, "With all this horse shit, there must be a horse in here somewhere!"

The reason for telling this story is simple. We have to look for the good in every situation, for if we look hard enough, we will succeed in finding it! Even when the situation involves our parents, we should try to be like the boy playing in the horse patties and see the "potential good" in every situation. *Although there is an interesting parallel between our parents and the room with horse manure, I assure you it is only a coincidence!*

During my freshman year at the University of Pennsylvania, my friends and I were sitting around discussing our home life. In the middle of the conversation, a friend asked me how my "rents" were doing. I didn't know how to answer. Quite frankly, I didn't know what "rents" meant.

2

Could "rents" be some growth that needed to be cut or burnt off? Or worse, something that could be cured with a shot of penicillin! (For those readers who are like me and have no formal medical training, penicillin is a common drug used to cure sexually transmitted diseases. I know this because I READ it.)

Unfortunately, and not due to the lack of "trying," I had not had the opportunity to participate in any sexual activity that might require a shot of penicillin, so this was definitely out.

I finally asked my friend. His reply proved to be worse than all of my imagined definitions above, as "rents" is short for "parents."

So, whenever "rent" is used, it is a nickname for "parent," and "rents" or "the rents" is plural for "parents."

Now, let's get down to business.
QUESTION: What do you want out of your relationship with your parents?

If you don't know what I mean by this question, let me lend you a hand, for the rest of this book will only help you if you have a clearly defined answer. Do you only want material things like more clothes, a stereo, a new car? How about a conversation over dinner without a war breaking out? Do you want your rents to listen to your thoughts and ideas? Possibly, you only want to be left alone?

For me, the answer to this question is all of the above. I would also like to have a relationship with my parents where we are friends and can speak openly with each other while the other party *actually* listens. *You know, where we are not interrupted and constantly told what to do.* The bottom line is -- I want more control over my life so I can do as I please without my parents getting in the way. Furthermore, when we are together, I simply want everyone to have a good time.

Write down what you want from your parents in the following space.

In order to understand how to have a good relation-ship with our parents, we really need to understand what a relationship is! Here is my own definition of a *relationship:* **A state of tolerance in which we and our parent(s) can spend time together under agreeable terms. The most important values which must be present for the relationship to work are TRUST and HONESTY** *and a very very large allowance. (The allowance part is not a necessity, but it sure helps!)*

Now, totally ignore the definition above and just remember two things: #1) **trust** and **honesty** must be a part of a healthy relationship; and #2) most parents believe in number #1 above.

4

Let's quickly define TRUST and HONESTY:

TRUST is being true to any commitment we or our parents make, following through to fulfill our word. This is fundamental to any relationship, for without trust, there is doubt, insincerity, and distrust, all of which are destructive to the relationship.

HONESTY is simply **telling the truth.** If any person in a relationship lies or intentionally hides the truth, they damage the relationship.

I cannot stress how important TRUST and HONESTY are to a relationship.

Now I know the subject of trust and honesty is about as exciting as a trip to the dentist's office -- but there's not much more, so hang with me.
If you can truly understand everything in the next paragraph, you are on your way toward managing your rents!

Trust and honesty are not instantly felt by everyone in a relationship, but must slowly develop over time. This means that we need to create a track record without deviation from total honesty and trustworthiness. Any breach of trust or honesty will create a sense of "doubt" and damage the relationship. When this happens, it will take more time and effort to reestablish feelings of trust and honesty within the relationship than it originally took to create the relationship.

Of course these two attributes apply to us and our parents equally. For example: Your mom and dad told you that they would lend you the car Saturday. All of

5

your friends are waiting at their homes for you to pick them up, but your parents jerk your chain and decide that they need the car. (Although a relationship is damaged when trust is broken by accident, a relationship is damaged even more when trust is intentionally broken.)

You are screwed and it is an understatement to say that your friends are not very happy with you.

At 3:00 in the afternoon, the "happy couple" drive up to the house. They get out of the car wearing golf clothes, carrying golf clubs, and drinking beers.

When you tell them, "Mom/Dad, you promised that I could use the car today!" they reply, "We're sorry, but grandma isn't feeling well and we had to go visit her."

You know that they are lying. What are you feeling? *Personally, I would like to take their clubs and wrap them around their heads and then put their golf bags where the sun doesn't shine!* Not only did they break their word about lending you the car, but they lied about what they have really done.

How does this incident affect future dealings with your parents? The next time they promise to lend you the car, will you trust them? Will you believe them when they tell you where they have been or what they have been doing? Most importantly, if your parents can break their word and then lie to you so easily, how much do they really care about you?

The point is, if you have any doubt about what your own parents tell you, this SUCKS and severely damages your relationship. Your parents, in not keeping their word and then lying to you, have hurt you and themselves. It only has to happen once!

How many times have your parents burned you by being untrustworthy or dishonest? How many times have you been untrustworthy or dishonest with them? If either you or one of your parents has broken either value, then that person is the sphincter who has weakened your relationship.

Unfortunately, in the majority of cases where there is a breach of trust or honesty between us and our parents, it is my opinion that WE are the guilty party.

VERY IMPORTANT: *Don't get rattled!* Parents are the most forgiving people in the world. Regardless of what we have done in the past, as long as we re-dedicate ourselves to the relationship by being honest and trustworthy, it can be rebuilt.

Now, let's fantasize that our parents believe and trust us. How would our situation be different? First, our parents will be more trusting with their belongings. *For my sister, it was my Mom's clothing. For a stud like me, it was the car. (If you really believe I'm a stud, I would like to sell you some beautiful swamp land.)* These items are extremely important possessions to any parent. Perks and rewards are given for trustworthiness and responsible behavior.

Second, when we do not lie, anything we say in a

conversation with the rents is more credible, especially when we really need their undivided attention or some serious help. No longer will we be treated like the boy who cried, "Wolf!"

For the unfamiliar, this is the story about a young shepherd boy who wanted to get some attention, so he lied over and over by crying out that there was a "Wolf." One day when the boy was tending his sheep, a real wolf actually did appear. *Upon soiling his skivvies,* the boy again cried "wolf," but no one in the town believed him. *After all, why should they?* The rest is obvious, as the wolf ate the little dweeb for lunch.

Ultimately, total honesty leads to a closer relationship with our parents since we will be able to communicate better and do what we want. No longer will they look for our deceptions. Believe me, this is all parents really want from us: the ability to be near us and have a close RELATIONSHIP.

If you have any doubts, the following two lists are proof:

What Our Parents Give and Do For Us:	**What We Give and Do For Our Parents:**
love	love
time	amusement
attention	chores
money	affection
help when we need it	help if they need it?
amusement	appreciation?
food	pride in us?
shelter	attention?
education	emotional support?
money	*grey hair?*
clothing	*ulcers ?*
vacations	*debt ?*
emotional support	*hemorrhoids?*
medical care	*gas?*
money	

Looking at the lists, you really begin to wonder why our parents even bothered to have us. I guess the lists prove two things: first, parents want to spend quality time with us, and second, rents really are morons. The good time they had while conceiving us has become very costly, especially since they could have enjoyed the event without any of the long-term responsibilities!

Seriously, all our parents want from us is time, attention, love, appreciation, and the effort to perform to the best of our ability. Everything else is really secondary. When we take more than we give, we are not being fair. *You know as well as I, that our parents know when we are being selfish.* At that very moment when we unfairly take advantage of them, they feel abused and somehow will get even with us. *And do they know how to get even!*

If we help fulfill our parents' needs and desires, they will reciprocate. This give and take is fair and it creates a good relationship in which everyone benefits!

That's all for chapter 1!

Multiple Choice Questions (choose the best response):

Because each of our parents loves and cares more about us than any other person:
   A. we can be cruel and unfeeling.
   B. we can speak to them rudely.
   C. we can take unfair advantage of them.
   D. All of the above.
   E. None of the above, and if you think any of the above answers are appropriate, you may need to re-examine how you treat your parents.

Because each of our parents loves and cares more about us than any other person:

A. we can trust them so that they will trust us.
B. we should be nice to them so that they will be nice to us.
C. we should not take unfair advantage of them so that they treat us fairly.
D. we should try to treat them like friends and confidants so that they do the same.
E. All of the above.

Because I have always hated having to flip to another page in a book for answers, **the correct answer for each question and all future multiple choice questions is the last letter option.** If you feel another letter is more appropriate, you should examine what part of your relationship with your parents makes you feel this way and how you can change it, *if you so wish.*

Chapter 2: Have Your Cake and Eat It Too!

Wouldn't you like to have a relationship with your parents and enjoy all the potential advantages of being their child? If you would, you have to decide at some point (hopefully soon), that to have a good relationship with your parents, you need to voluntarily share what is happening in your life. This includes your feelings, beliefs, doubts, fears, etc.. It also includes being open and honest with your parents, always keeping your word, and never lying.

There are some skeptics reading this book who think they could never be open and honest with their parents and that I must be loopy. They feel that if their parents really knew the truth about some of the things they did, not only would they be tarred and feathered, but they would be imprisoned in their room for about forty years. What, it would be worse than that?!? They would be locked up without the use of a T.V., a telephone, and have to listen to Barry Manilow all day and night. This sounds pretty inhumane! Well, they might be right, but I would not be wasting my time writing this book if I truly believed that this was a real concern, so keep reading and have an open mind.

The secret to not being punished and having an open and honest relationship with your parents is to make them **NOT want** to punish you. Here are some examples of how you can make this happen:

The first technique is the direct approach: Decide which parent is easier to talk to and has influence over the other. *We all know which rent that is.*

Simply walk up to that parent and say, "How about

you and I forming an agreement?" *When they ask what you are babbling about, respond,* "When I tell you the absolute truth, you won't punish me." *If they say, "no," remind them about George Washington cutting down his father's cherry tree. When George Washington was asked by his dad if he had done it, since he told the truth and said, "yes," he was not punished. (For those of you who failed history, the George Washington was our first President, had wooden teeth, and knew how to make Martha blush like a school girl, if you know what I mean!)*

Don't give up! Keep pushing your rents to at least try your suggestion. Eventually, they will say, "YES."

For those of you who want to make sure that you have covered your butt, ask your parents if they would put their promise in writing. If they say anything other than,"YES," say something like, "So that we won't have any **misunderstandings** later on, I will only feel comfortable if we both back up our words in writing!"

Now, I'm not a lawyer, but the first contract in the back of this book is a document that I have drafted for you and your parents to sign (feel free to make copies of it). It should make them feel more comfortable while it also covers your derriere!

The second technique to convince your parents not to punish you when you tell them the truth is the method I used:

Go to that same parent when they are alone and get their attention by explaining that you have something very important to tell them, but can't. Being curious to hear what you have to say, your rent will ask,"why not?" Now explain that you can't tell them because they will punish you.

Your parent will probably either deny your statement about punishing you when you are open and honest, *in which case you should recite the many incidents when you have been punished for telling the truth* or, they may try to *rock your boat* and force the truth out of you.

No matter what they do or the consequences of what they tell you, stick to your guns and do not tell them anything until they have agreed NOT to punish you. Even if they threaten punishments in order to make you tell them the truth, tell them **NOTHING!** Accept the punishment; it will be worth it!

Something else you might say is: "Mom/Dad, I always want to tell you the truth and communicate openly, but if I tell you what happened last night, I will probably be rewarded with a punishment." *Now you must ask them a loaded question which will make them really think:* "Do you really think a punishment is a good incentive for telling the truth, because if you do, you will never hear what happened last night." *Slowly head toward the door so that you can get "OUT"' should the time come to escape.*

Again, **do not reveal any of the information they want to hear unless they agree to NO PUNISHMENT.** *By keeping your word, they will respect your determination and admire you for having enough guts to confront them. Of course, they won't let you know this.*

The next time you state that you will not tell them something without their guarantee of no punishment, they will know that you mean business and will be more likely to give in to your proposal.

Here is what happened when I used this technique:

Since my Mother is a little more than slightly neurotic, she immediately wanted to know what I had to tell her and was willing to promise just about anything!

I was more than pleased, but knew my Father all too well! When he heard the story from her, unless I had her absolute support, he would put my ass in a sling. (That's why the

I PROMISE I'LL NEVER PUNISH YOU AGAIN — PLEASE SHARE YOUR THOUGHTS WITH ME !

Well, If you insist . . . .

parent you first talk to has to be able to control the other parent.) I simply told her that she had to promise that neither she nor my Dad would cause any punishment for anyone involved, especially myself, now or in the future.

This caught her pretty flat-footed, as parents can be all too creative when it comes to handing out punishments. *(You have to cover your ass when managing parents. It does come with practice.)* She hesitated, smiled, and then agreed.

At this point, I told my Mom that although I hadn't tried marijuana, I had seen it for the first time with some of my friends. Her expression was so astounding

that I can't even describe it!   I just wish I had had a camera!

(The best part is that she so badly wanted to punish me in all kinds of evil ways, but was not even able to touch me. It was awesome!)

Then when she heard the whole story, she took a dozen Valium and drank a fifth of vodka. No, that's just a joke. She actually took the whole affair pretty calmly, considering!

From that point on, getting her to promise not to punish me became easier and easier, until a general agreement was made between my parents and me that no punishments would be given when I told the truth.

Well, now you have the tools to build honest communication with your parents without the fear of being punished. When you use them, you will have taken your first step to a better relationship and life.

Building Trust is the next task. Trust can only be developed over time, as you simply have to prove to your parents consistently, time and time again, that **what you say you will do, you do.**

What? Did someone comment that since your parents ask for totally unreasonable things that when you don't follow through, your parents will lose faith in you? Here's how to handle this problem:

1) Fully understand exactly what your parents are asking of you; and 2) If you have any doubts about whether or not you will actually do something, tell your parents with honest communication that their expectations might not get fulfilled and why.

If what they ask of you really is reasonable, then you don't have any excuse to break their trust. *We all know what is reasonable or not, and if we don't give in to the rents sometimes, how can we receive?* If, however, their request is unreasonable, *as parents have been known to be,* you must negotiate what will be done, how it will be done, and when it will be done, etc. *Don't worry, tactics and techniques in negotiating are revealed in Chapter 8.*

After negotiations are finished and you promise that something will be done, **you must follow through!** VERY IMPORTANT: Do NOT say you will do something if you know you will NOT or cannot do it! Re-negotiate until you can fulfill your promise or simply state, "Because I don't want to break my word to you, I want to tell you up front that I can not promise that what you want me to do will be totally fulfilled. **All I can do is to try my best."**

I'll get the mop...

When parents hears this rational and honest statement, they will probably be so overjoyed that they will "wet their pants" and agree to your new terms. After they do agree, don't laugh in their faces, just give them a diaper and a mop for any puddle they may have made.

By being open and honest, you can survive your parents without losing their trust in you. Most importantly, as your parents gain trust in you, they will be more inclined to give you **more freedom and privacy.**

Here's a little event in my life that I bet almost everyone can relate to in one way or another: When I was about twelve years old, my parents' confidence and trust in me had reached a remarkably high level. All of a sudden, I became afraid that I would have to lie to them, since a friend had brought some small bottles of liquor (the type they serve on airplanes) to a party. Since I'm a good friend, I couldn't let him finish it all by himself!

When confronted by my parents about drinking, I decided to tell the truth and wait for their verdict. By the time the jury finally came to a decision, I had figuratively bitten off all my fingernails and was working on my toenails (how limber I was back then!).

They began their verdict by telling me their usual, "Your mother and I have discussed it, and we feel that. . . (I couldn't believe the words that came out of their mouths!) you are old enough and responsible enough to experiment with alcohol, but only at home. We also want to know what you do." (Can you believe this?) They gave me a prized possession, the key to their liquor closet (maybe the most coveted possession next to a good fake I.D.). As long as the alcohol which my friends and I drank was replaced, I could drink their alcohol. (They told me of a liquor company which I could call to replace my consumption, at their expense -- not too bad huh?)

I had to be the luckiest kid in the world, as my parents' liquor cabinet had about a thousand times more liquor than the half-full bottle of rum hidden in my closet. Immediately, I opened their cabinet with the many glistening bottles of beautifully colored hooch (what a rush I felt!) and started to take an order of the upcoming weekend's cocktails.

That Friday night, my cousin and I mixed a huge pitcher of orange blossoms (put O.J., gin, powdered sugar and ice in a blender and then blend until the ice is finely crushed) and returned absolutely wasted. I had never realized that the world could spin so fast! When *my parents got home later that night and saw us, they laughed. This really pissed me off, especially when I asked why they were laughing and they told me I would find out the next morning. I'm sure it never even crossed their pea-sized brains to suggest that we should take some aspirin before going to sleep.*

The next morning, I woke up with two tennis players playing tennis in my room using my brain as the ball! A hang-over, what a horrible feeling. I promised Providence that if the pain ever went away, never, ever, again would alcohol touch my lips. (To this date, I wonder how many times this promise has been made?) When my cousin and I both staggered into the kitchen, my parents started laughing and asked how we liked drinking; then they laughed some more.

A great way to help build trust between you and your parents is to use the second contract in the back of the book. It may also help prevent a tragedy caused by drinking and driving. Look it over. You may like it or

18

you may not, but in either case, you might consider making a copy of it to give to a friend you care about. It could actually save someone's life.

That's all for chapter 2. I hope it has shown how we shouldn't underestimate the importance of honesty and trust. With trust and honesty as the basis of our relationship, we can get away with murder and are on the road to managing our parents.

Answer the following True or False:

1. Parents want us to tell the truth.
2. We want to tell the truth.
3. Parents want to be able to give us punishments even if we tell the truth.
4. We do not like to be punished for telling the truth.
5. We need to convince our parents that they cannot punish us when we tell the truth (that they can NOT have their cake and eat it too).
6. Our parents need to realize that if they want a good relationship with us, it must be based on honesty.
7. Our parents can be influenced to believe that hearing the truth from us is more important than the freedom to punish us.
8. If we can tell the truth without blame or punishment, our relationship with our parents will improve.
9. If handled subtly and with tact, we can get our parents to agree to NOT punish us for telling the truth.
10. We can use the first contract on in the back of the book to help fulfill our goal.

All of the above True/False questions should be answered True. If you have felt that any are false, evaluate what aspect of the question is false and why. Then determine how you can change your life so that the answer can become true, *if you wish to do so.*

Answer the following questions True or False:

1. Our parents want to trust us.
2. We want to trust our parents.
3. Parents can be overbearing and expect so much from us that they, in effect, force us to break their trust.
4. We can be lazy sacks of manure, not wanting to pull our own fair share.
5. We need to convince our parents to be reasonable in their demands and expectations of us.
6. We need to be fair to our parents by meeting some of their needs and demands.
7. We and our rents can discuss and then agree to what is expected of everyone.
8. Once our parents agree to do something they must fulfill their obligation.
9. Once we have agreed to do something, we will fulfill our obligation.
10. The contract regarding responsibility to not drive while under the influence is a tool we can use to demonstrate that we are trustworthy and that we want to work with our parents.

Again, all of the above True/False questions should be answered True. If you have felt that any are false, evaluate what aspect of the question is false and why. Then determine how you can change your life so that the answer can become true, *if you wish to do so.*

Chapter 3: How Our Parents Look At Us

*This chapter explains why our parents sometimes act like the snapperheads that they are. It will also show you how to take advantage of their many weaknesses, but with moderation. Hell, let's face facts, taking advantage of the rents in moderation is like being **partially** pregnant -- it's impossible! You are going to love this chapter!*

Parents have children for dozens of reasons. Some reasons are good and some absolutely stink. *My sister always told me that our parents really didn't want me. She later changed her story and told me that they did want me, but since I was born a girl and they already had one, they had me changed into a boy. It is embarrassing to tell this story, especially since I actually believed her until I was eight years old!*

Parents try to guide our growth and development according to their own beliefs so that we become what they perceive to be a "good person." *(just like them!)* As a result, there are many ways in which they will influence our lives both positively and negatively.

The first and most obvious method is through their own actions. For instance, parents tend to act differently when they are around us than when they are alone with their friends or they may act particularly proper in front of us so that we will pick up good habits and not the bad ones. Furthermore, when we are young, parents usually refrain from using any bad language around us, *unless they become overly-excited, in which case they sometimes use this "bad language" at us.*

Other areas in which they will try to guide or influence us are our values, our education, our religious, political, social, moral beliefs and much, much more. *You know, all those wonderful, fantastic, and earthshaking qualities of being a "respected" member of society, as well as becoming a pillar of mankind just like our angelic parents!*

As a result of our parent's influence, we usually end up with characteristics similar to one or both of them. Hence, the horrible, but often true saying, "the apple doesn't fall far from the tree." *Fortunately, in my case, I'm an exception to the "apple theory," for I think my parents came from the prune family.*

Of course you probably already knew all of the trash above, as your parents have undoubtedly told you again and again what a great job they are doing with your development, what a difficult a job parenting is, and all of the abundantly complicated reasons why they have raised you as they have.

Let's look at other reasons why rents behave as they do. Let's examine the real motives which they will never admit or even acknowledge as influencing factors.

While our parents are making us do what *they think* is "best" for us, they often will be partaking in these events or be there watching us. *Did I hear you ask "Why?"* The reasons for their actions are:

1) To amuse themselves. *Yes, our parents are amused by us.* It may be hard to believe, but we are here partly to amuse, surprise, excite *and to take the boredom out of our parents' otherwise boring lives.* Parents get to play with us, watch us, teach us, scream at us, beat us, *just getting a little carried away,* in excitement or in anger, and laugh and cry with us. We keep them amused and on their toes.

22

Even though they pretend not to like surprises, don't let them fool you. Parents love to be surprised.

Those little surprises are always remembered!

Have you ever heard them say, "That boy (or that girl) is something else!"? Though their expression sounds exasperated, they really are amused and very happy. We keep them young, alive, and energetic. Our generation is their future. *Boy are they in trouble!* Our parents take care of us and then we take care of them.

2) To live vicariously through us. Living "vicariously" through us, is just a regular old pastime for parents. A good example of how rents "live vicariously" or "relive" their life through us is the following: A father who never played football in high school, but wishes he had, influences his son to play. He never misses his son's football games.

At the game, he screams, cheers and runs around telling everyone who his son is. *You know the guy I'm talking about, the old fool that runs around looking as*

23

stupid as gumby! The father is reliving his youth, a part that he missed by not playing football himself.

Another example is a mother pressuring her daughter to be popular because she was not popular herself when she was young.

Here is a personal example: *From my birth, possibly even before my birth, it was expected that I would attend the same business school that my dad had attended. When I was actually accepted to the University of Pennsylvania, my father was happier than I. (My dad attended many, many years ago, sometime around the stone age. It is amazing how rents hate to discuss their age. Someone should tell them that being older than fifty is not that old -- at least not for an oak tree.)*

Finally, my mother always wanted both of her children to play the piano because she never took lessons herself. As a result, she made my sister and me take about eight years of lessons between us! To this day, neither my sister nor I play the piano, nor do we care care to play the piano. Mom, if you want to play the piano, take the lessons yourself -- and don't forget to practice at least thirty minutes a day!

It is truly amazing how parents will try to force us to do what they did as children, and also what they did not do as children, but now wish that they had. They do this to satisfy their own needs and to help build their self-esteem. This may include sometimes acting like hypocrites in expecting us to do something that they themselves have never done! *I guess we just have to accept that parents are the world's biggest hypocrites.*

Unfortunately, parents are usually not even aware that they are making us unhappy when they make us do things we do not want to do. All they know is that since they are happy, it must be what is "best" for us and also what makes us happy. Hard to believe?

But we are not helpless!

To counter our parents' propensity for grand expectations, try to understand and discuss these expectations with your parents. This open communication will help to let them know your feelings as well as to better understand what their personal motivation(s) actually are (and possibly even tone down their expectations).

It is necessary, however, to differentiate between a parent's living vicariously through us via extracurricular activities and their desiring to teach us skills for "survival." Reading, writing, math, etc. are all necessities for basic survival.

When parents push us to excel in these and other essential areas, they only want what is truly best for us. As long as the pressures placed on us by our parents are constructive and are reasonable, we should actually feel proud and appreciative that they care so much!

Here are some helpful ideas to chew on: Our parents often judge the success of their parenting by how much we believe in and follow their values, interests, actions, and beliefs. When we try to be ourselves and this conflicts with their values, interests, actions, and beliefs, we are threatening their feeling of being "good parents."

So, in order to maintain their feelings of being "good parents," they often try to control us and force their ideas and values into our heads.

But let's get to the point. The key is to remove the pressures our parents put on themselves to be good parents by simply telling them that we think they are "terrific parents" and "terrific people" and that even though we may differ from them in certain ways, we appreciate their allowing us to be "ourselves." *I know how tough it will be to tell your rents they are "terrific," but don't let your ego or pride prevent you from flattering your parents or you will be screwing yourself over!* After all, **WE** are the true critics to determine whether or not our parents are "good parents."

All right. Enough of this chapter!

Chapter 4: How We Should Look At Our Parents

I want you to put on a new pair of glasses, or better yet, I'm going to lend you my eyes for a while. When you have finished seeing your parents as I do mine, hopefully, you will see them in a new light.

It's totally amazing how we see our parents when we are really young. They are the "Ultimate Beings." Parents are so wise that they can see the future! They are the supreme rulers, only answering to a handful of others including our grandparents (who are even more all-knowing than our parents), a police officer (he carries a gun), the President of the United States, and finally, God. *In my family, my father sometimes gets confused with the latter.*

One day, like lightning striking, we realize that we are our own person and can explore the world as we wish. It is doing this and getting along with the parents that is such a pain in the butt. *They always seem to get in the way of what we want to do, and always at the worst times!*

Think back to first grade. When we were really young, we used the age of people to determine their intelligence, height, strength, and speed. Age was so important to us that when someone said we were "six" years old, we insisted that we were "six and a half" years old. My sister wasn't merely my older sister, but a big kid who was a couple of years older than I!

Being a meathead, I thought that when I got to be her age, I would be her equal. I finally reached the age of ten. Can you imagine, two digits to my age!

Unfortunately, my "big sister" was still older and she and her boyfriends had grown even bigger! I hadn't taken into consideration that they would be growing at the same rate that I was. I thought to myself, "Don't worry, just give it a few more years." What a mental pygmy I was, and I can proudly say that depending on whom you ask, things haven't changed much.

Well, eventually after many years and what seemed like an eternity, I caught up with them and now they say, "I can't believe you're Copey Pulitzer! I remember when. . ." My usual response to this is, " Please don't remind me."

Well, the point of the garbage above is to illustrate that just as I finally caught up with my sister and her friends, we eventually catch up with our parents.

It happens like this: At the relatively young age of six, our parents are so many times older than we are that we can't even begin to understand what it would be like to be thirty. They can drive a car and go anywhere they please. They don't even have to go to school! *We can't wait to grow up even though we should not rush it.* We perceive parents as having attained the supreme level of wisdom and physical growth, *which we eventually realize is all a bunch of crap.*

Parents will never admit to their flaws. *The real truth is that parents are overweight, their hair is either turning grey or falling out altogether, their gums will soon be supporting dentures instead of teeth, they are having sexual dysfunction, and they are just as confused about life as we are, but they fake it better.*

Stop and think for a second. A parent's physical appearance plays a strong role in our perception of them. Here's a personal example: *Throughout my life, when my Dad asked me to do something, it always held more authority than when Mom asked, especially when I*

28

was younger.

When comparing the physical attributes of men to women, since men have heavier and louder voices, a larger physical size, and since men are so much less attractive than women *(unless she was in the class of 1987 at the University Of Pennsylvania),* men are more

intimidating. *My father was much more intimidating!*

More over, my father's punishments were about a thousand times more painful than my Mom's. If he had a belt on during any discussion, he could pull it out for a "strapping" as he called it. (I can remember it all too vividly. When he pulled his belt off, it would make a sound that still causes a chill to run through my body. To this day, that sound fills me with a deep feeling of resentment! I know that I will never use a belt on my kids.)

Well, one day (I can't remember when or why), I

began to see my parents for who they are -- ordinary people. *It was like being hit by a Mack truck. I felt like a moron. Maybe even worse, a retarded moron.* I saw that they are far from perfect and that they make loads of mistakes just like me. *In fact, the reason they know so much about mistakes is that they have so much more experience in making them!*

It is often said that a true mistake is a mistake that is repeated. A mistake made only once is experience. *My parents are very experienced!* Furthermore, instead of being Mom and Dad, they became Joyce and Sid, two people with needs, desires, and aversions similar to mine.

And parents are not more special than we because of their age or acquired experience. On the contrary, we are more special than they, for we still have youth.

Now realization has set in and we see our parents as they truly are. But do we really? In order to maximize our ability to manage our parents, it is necessary to understand them **from their perspective.**

Here is how we can do this. Analyze the **needs** and **desires** of each parent separately and then analyze both parents as a pair. Parents as individuals have their own unique ideals, beliefs, values, characteristics, etc. Write down these needs and desires and try to rank them by what you feel their importance is to each parent and then to both parents. Some of these may be listed on page 8 in Chapter 1. Now make a list ranking the actions and beliefs that they dislike.

Look over all of these characteristics and get a feel for them. These qualities are the keys to managing your parents. If rents like something, use it as a positive incentive to get what you want. *Like candy to a baby, Mr. Kool-aid to a parched man in the desert or a breath freshener to a date with doggy breath.* If they dislike something, this is considered a negative motivator. *For example, if you want to get someone out of your car, the negative method to accomplish this is to pull over, close all of the windows, unlock the doors and then fart.*

Don't run off yet to manage your parents. Hold your horses. We have some ground work to cover first. Why do our parents act the way they do? What is the basis of their beliefs?

The first way to answer these questions is through our parents' parents, *otherwise known as grandparents.* Grandparents are a tremendous source of information about our parents since they know them better than anyone else. Examine your grandparents and the way they interact with your parents. Attempting to be as objective as you possibly can, try to figure out the basis of your parents and grandparents' relationship. *This is very easy, just be observant.*

For instance, here are some questions you may want to write down answers to:

1. How much love have your grandparents given your parents?
2. How have they shown this love?
3. How much attention have your grandparents given your parents?
4. Which grandparent is your Mom/Dad closer to and why? Why not the other?
5. Are they good friends, and if so, why? Why not?
6. Do they enjoy being together or do they fight a lot? Why?
7. Is your Mom/Dad the dominant party in the relationship and why? Why not?

Most importantly, try to distinguish how your Mom/Dad was raised by their own parents. How were they treated? Try to fit the answers to these questions to your own relationship with your parents.

You might find some similarities in the relationship between you and your parents as well as some totally opposing characteristics. The better you understand where each of your parents is coming from, the greater your ability to motivate them to your way of thinking or anticipate their reactions to any of your antics.

Some other unknowns that you should discover from your Mom's/Dad's relationship with their parents are:

1. Have your grandparents been understanding with your parents?
2. How do your grandparents and parents communicate together?
3. How do they communicate best? Worst? (under what conditions and in what way?)
4. How do they spend their time together?
5. What do your parents think of your grandparents and why?
6. What do your grandparents think of your parents and why?
7. What seem to be your grandparents' values, morals, outlooks, and are they similar to your parents'? What areas are different? Why?

Stop and really think about these questions. Which ones do you **NOT** have an answer to? Maybe there is a secret to be discovered!?! By answering a few of these questions, you will begin to see why your parents act the way they do.

Since I know you have gone through the questions

over and over and as thoroughly as you possibly can, now is the time to ask your grandparents questions. *Because grandparents are suckers for attention, they will usually answer any question.*

Find out from all of your grandparents, if possible, about the economic environment in which your parents were raised. *This is critical to understanding their feelings about money.* Find out about where your parents were raised, their health as a kid, their best friends. Try to discover if your rents were popular, how they did in school, what they did as a child, the troubles they got into, their fears, beliefs, etc..

Their answers will definitely give you a better perspective for evaluating your parents. Furthermore, you may be so amazed by some of the stories that your grandparents tell you that you may want to ask your parents a "probing" question or two.

In doing this, I found out that not only was my father punished by "strappings" and locked in their closet, but my grandfather was also punished by "strappings" when he grew up in an orphanage! Knowing this helped me to understand and deal with my dad.

Aunts and uncles can also help to answer questions as well as provide some real good low down stuff on your parents. . . For example: *I learned from my uncle that when my Dad was a kid, he used to operate on lizards. One day, Pops (what I call my Dad) decided he was ready for a greater challenge. Taking his little brother into his "operating room," he prepared for his ultimate leap into the world of medicine by giving him an appendectomy (remove his appendix). Supposedly, my father was just ready to commence his greatest scientific feat (one that I have no doubt would have been published in many a medical journal including "Ripley's Believe It or*

Not") when an adult blew his cover! He was busted!

To this day, Pops denies the whole thing. But I don't blame him, I would too!

We also need to evaluate what is currently going on in our parents' lives. Just as you inquire into their pasts, keep yourself up to date on current issues and events in their lives that affect them. This includes: their health, work, worries, concerns, fears, their own parents etc.. You can do this very easily by asking one parent about the other.

Sometimes we do not appreciate or realize what our parents constantly deal with in their lives, especially after they have children -- us. When first married, our parents enjoyed a simple life with little responsibility, living fancy free and having a great time.

Then, from enjoyable, carefree lives, their lives change to "organized chaos" when they have a child who constantly cries, must regularly be fed and messes in its diapers. No longer can they just pick up, go out at night, *and come back home in their horny moods, doing "it" on the kitchen or dining room table.*

34

Now, the rents must start saving money in order to pay for their new financial burden -- us. As the number of kids increases, so do our parents' responsibilities, worries, and problems.

With more people to support, their financial burden grows. Every month, there is:

> a mortgage/rent on the house
> payments on the car
> payments for car insurance
> food bills
> clothing bills
> books and education bills
> electrical bills
> telephone bills
> doctor bills
> entertainment expenses

Frustrations and concerns also build for our parents, including:
>stress at work (keeping the boss happy and
>>their jobs intact)
>potential marital problems (keeping the
>>flame alive or dating if single)
>declining health *or growing love handles*
>preparation for their future retirement
>us, including our health, our general well-being
>>and the constant problems we bring to
>>their attention.
>free time for themselves
>keeping the house clean
>preparing meals
>driving us around
>all of the emotions of frustration, jealousy,
>>anger, and fear that they feel with their
>>own friends (many of the same emotions
>>we may feel with our friends)
>*keeping the lint out of their bellybuttons*

*These are some serious problems! Personally, I
think I prefer the idea of living fancy free and "spending
more time around the kitchen table!"*

These lists add up to stress, so when parents are
tired, frazzled, and generally "stressed out," let them
have their own space. Be understanding, as parents
have a lower tolerance for our BS (bullshit) when they
are "uptight." After all, it's only fair. Our parents do
have a life of their own *just like all other mushrooms
and spoors in the fungi family.* Their purpose in life is
not simply to serve our needs and wants. *(I have left a
space for your own witty response to the last sentence.)*

When dealing with your parents, try to have a posi-

36

tive attitude. *It also helps so you won't get nauseous.*
Often, a parent's worrying or anger is actually **love** and
caring just expressed in a way that we take as nosy or
demanding. Don't get upset or angry by their worrying.
Just accept it for what it really is, and try to mitigate
their worries by coming up with ways to put their fears
to rest.

Another way to look at your parents' worrying is to
pretend that a close friend has said what your parent
just did. For example, if a friend said, "Be careful driving, the streets are wet," or "Fasten your seat belt," you
would feel appreciation and warmth toward them for
caring. Why shouldn't we feel the same appreciation
and warmth toward our parents?

*The following is so deep that I have to read it twice
to understand it and I'm the one who wrote it! To tell the
truth, I scare myself sometimes.*

Parents as parents "need to be needed" by us. They
also use "rewards" and "punishments" to motivate us.
As we get older, these "rewards" and "punishments"
become meaningless to us and no longer work in controlling our actions, thoughts, desires, etc.. *You know this is
happening when their threats become meaningless.*
Furthermore, the fact that we want to be more indepen-
dent and don't want to "need" our parents as much as in
the past puts an even greater tension on them.

When all this happens, they can go loco, regarding
the change in us as "rebelling" or at least as being "difficult." As a result, they can "flip out" and in the process,
say and do very foolish things.

Here is how to deal with the above chain-reaction:
As we get older, we have to show our parents that
we still need them, but in a different way. We want to

be treated as friends on an **equal** basis; we want to be dealt with as people, not their property. In response to their emotional outbursts, we must stay under control, keeping our cool and explaining to them that we are not trying to rebel against them, but are trying to find out who and what we are. *If this doesn't work, try a colonic enema to cool them down.*

If we want more freedom and decision-making power over our lives, we must actually get **closer** to our parents and, *believe it or not,* **not** push them away. To achieve our goal, we have to show them that we are "mature" and "responsible," have good judgement, are honest, reliable, and trustworthy. *Believe it or not, when parents consistently see this, you may find that they will voluntarily give you the freedom and autonomy that you desire.*

The worst thing we can do is daydream about having perfect parents, as there is no such thing and we cannot live in a daydream. Trying to do so can lead to unhappiness for everyone!

Finally, remember to have a positive attitude and don't take your parents or even yourself too seriously. Sometimes, we have the choice of either laughing or crying about a problem. This is an easy decision, since laughter is much more enjoyable. *It's like playing bare foot in the back yard with your friends and stepping in a fresh steaming pile of dog-poo. You have the option of cursing and letting everyone laugh at you, or you can laugh yourself while you take your nasty foot and smear it on the unsuspecting person next to you.* Laughing when you are down makes you feel better, and if you look hard enough, you will find or create something positive out of the situation.

38

Chapter 5: Listening

Some wise ass is asking himself why I have put a chapter on listening in this book. I would like to answer in three parts: 1) because this is my book and I want to; 2) because if you want a healthy relationship with anyone, you must have good communication and this means truly understanding how to LISTEN; and 3) refer to number 1, above.

Let's start from the top. Here is your first new skill and tool to use with your rents.

Active Listening

One of the most important aspects of communicating, developed and defined by Dr. Thomas Gordon in his book for our parents on how to handle us kids, PARENT EFFECTIVENESS TRAINING *(I've got to give credit where credit is due)* is "Active Listening." When the principles in Active Listening are followed, **the speaker appreciates and feels good about talking to the listener and the listener fully understands what the speaker has expressed.**

This is especially important when dealing with parents, for parents really respect our judgement when we "hear them out." *Besides, rents truly believe that everything that comes out of their mouths is soooo important. As a result, if we show respect by listening, they feel that we must respect them.*

To use **Active Listening:**

1.   Do not speak, make any distracting noise, or even open our mouth. Just listen without any interruption.

DO NOT INTERRUPT!

2.   Keep eye contact to show the speaker that we care and are paying attention.

3.   Every now and then, make small comments like "uh huh," "really," "wow," "let's hear it", "I'm listening," "I'd like to hear more," "let's discuss it," nodding our head, or even grunting to signify that we are listening. *In other words, don't scream, "Boring!"*

4.   Most important! Think about what we have heard and then repeat back to the speaker, in our own words, what we understood them to have said, including their feelings and intentions. This is an important test to signify that we have listened and truly understood what the speaker is trying to express to us.

If you can master this section, you will probably never again hear your parents say, "you never listen to me," or "why are you so damn hard headed?" Well, maybe not the last statement.

The most important aspect of all the numbers above is the one in bold print, #4. You must understand what your speaker's message is, what their feelings are and then accurately **reflect** their feelings back to them. An example of something you might say to a rent after Active Listening is called a "YOU" statement, such as:

"Dad, **you** feel. . .(upset over Uncle Bob's illness)."

"Mom, **you** mean to tell me that. . .(you are frustrated with your job)."

"Dad, **you** think. . .(your friend takes advantage of you)."

or probably, more appropriately:

*"Mom, **you** seem upset that you are getting as fat as a stuffed pig."*

*"Dad, **you** sound frustrated that you have more hair under your armpits than on your head."*

Once Active Listening is mastered, people will enjoy talking to you because you are a good listener.

Now let's see how well I have explained Active Listening. Here is a pop quiz:

Your mom is dressed to go out and accidentally rips her stockings. She looks at you and says, "I've changed my mind, you can not go out or use the car tonight." To signify that you understand her feelings and to get your privileges back you should:

A. laugh at her.

B. tell her that she is clumsy and then laugh at her.

C. tell her that she looks better with ripped stockings, that she is clumsy and then laugh at her.

D. say, "You seem upset that you messed up your stockings. Can I do anything to help?"

Your grandmother is ill and your dad seems flustered and in a bad mood. You should use Active Listening by stating:

A. You seem concerned about grandma.
B. Are you feeling alright?
C. Is there anything I can do for you?
D. All of the above.

The best answer is the last letter option.

Listen To Body Language

Body language is great for dealing with the opposite sex, our friends, and our parents. With this said, I sincerely hope you use body language as it is killer!

Of all the different types of body language, facial expressions like smiling, laughing, and crying are the easiest to read and become acquainted with. When someone's eyes look teary, they are probably upset or very touched. If their eyes are blinking a lot, it can mean that they are attentive to whatever they are doing. If someone's eyes are glassy, red, or unfocused, it could mean that they are tired, or they could be on some type of medication.

Another aspect to observe is a person's coloring (the color in their face). When a person's face is redder than normal, they may be embarrassed or angry. If a person's face is unnaturally pale, they can be tired or frightened.

If you are observant, a person's hands also send out signals. The most obvious body signal is a closed hand with an extended middle finger, *A.K.A (also known as) "the bird."*

Other "hand messages" include: When someone's hands move a lot and/or they touch their hands to their face, they may be excited, nervous, or uptight. If their hands shake, they may be excited or possibly they just drank too much the night before (the D.T.'s). When a person's hands are stationary and calm, that person usually is comfortable and relaxed.

A person's posture can also tell a story. A person sitting back in a chair with their feet comfortably placed is probably relaxed. On the other hand, if they are sitting on the edge of their chair and leaning into the conversation, they are probably alert and attentive. When you are talking to someone and their body suddenly changes position, the topic you have just mentioned may be a sensitive one. The best way to understand what someone is feeling is to ask yourself what you would be feeling if you positioned your own body in the exact same way.

Body Language Quiz:
You and your class have taken a trip together over the Christmas Holidays and you are visiting a girl you like in her hotel room. She is sitting in a chair with one of her legs tucked under her tush (I have never understood why women sit this way). With her other foot, she is playing with her shoe by dangling it on her toes and flipping it around. *She is showing you through her body language that she is relaxed with you.* Now that you are aware of body language, you observe that her shoe has "accidentally" fallen off of her foot, but she has not made any attempt to put it back on. Instead, she is smiling at you with a special twinkle in her eyes. Question: What is her body language telling you now?

Answer: Merry Christmas!

When dealing with parents, try to read their body language to determine how best to approach them. For example, if your rents are visibly agitated, annoyed, angry, etc., approach them very cautiously! Finally, the more you try to read body language, the better you get, so when negotiating or *playing poker,* be observant.

It Can't Hurt To Listen To Knowledge
and Experience

I will have you know that I was not bribed by my parents to include this section.

Although we do not have to follow a person's advice, it never hurts to hear what they have to say **and then make our own decision.** This is especially true of someone who is trusted and has more experience and knowledge than we, like our parents. Maybe their advice is total garbage *(it probably is)* or maybe it is terrific, will bring insight to a situation, and helps us to avoid a mistake *(very doubtful)*.

Here is what my parents are like: Often after my parents have given me advice, they expect me to obey their ideas without a moment's hesitation or thought. If I didn't jump high enough to satisfy their expectations, they just assumed I was not listening or did not understand them. Has this ever happened to you?!?

Instead of just telling the rents that their opinion sucks or that they are totally out of their minds, try some of the tricks I use when I don't agree with what my parents tell me:

1. "The Honest Approach"

I restate their message in my own words and then say something like: "Mom/Dad, I heard and understand what you have said, but I **respectfully** (a very important word to help maintain a parent's self esteem) disagree." Then I state my reason(s) and feelings for disagreeing.

2. "The Compromise"

I try at least to incorporate some aspect of their suggestion, no matter how insignificant or minuscule it may be, into whatever I decide to do. Then I make a big deal out of following their advice.

3. "The Silent Kiss Off"

I just thank them for caring enough to share their opinion and their tremendous efforts on my behalf. Then I simply do what I want. *It is literally a "silent kiss-off," and it works!*

My parents have saved me from much self-inflicted pain, frustration, mistakes, and wasted time by giving me good advice. Almost as important as the advice is the appreciation and respect parents feel when we **ask** for their opinions *(even if we know we are NOT going to follow their suggestions!)! The bottom line is -- parents love being heard and we love doing what we want. Everyone wins!*

Chapter 6: Expressing Ideas and Feelings

Now, let's discuss the flip side of listening, expressing our ideas and feelings so that the listener understands our message. Good communication with parents is expressing our feelings toward them so that they truly understand how much we love and care for them. It is expressing how we want to spend "quality time" with them that is enjoyable for everyone.

Letters

The first and easiest method to help us build communication with our parents is writing them letters which express our feelings. Whether a letter is good or bad, happy or sad, loving or resentful, etc., it prevents direct confrontation and we are better able to convey our point of view without getting interrupted, confused, or losing control of the situation. *Do not forget to write some good, happy and loving letters.*

Letters also alleviate a lot of the pressures that a parent feels during a skirmish. Because letters do not put parents "on the spot," they can remain calm and reply with their own letter that expresses

Dear Dad,
I think having your nose pierced is the way to go.
Love,
your Son,
Spike

their own feelings and thoughts.

Most importantly, when we and our rents are able to express ourselves in a more peaceful manner, everyone benefits.

HOW We Communicate With Our Parents

How we communicate with anyone, especially our parents, is just as important as **what** we say! Expressing feelings, opinions, and ideas **in a positive way** will strengthen our message.

Remember how we used "YOU" messages in Active Listening to check the speaker's feelings and intentions (number 4 of Active listening "you must feel. . .")? Well, when we are trying to express OUR opinions and feelings, we should use "I" messages (another idea espoused by Dr. Thomas Gordon). An "I" message allows us to voice our opinions within the confines of our own feelings so that we don't attack our listener. *If we use "I" messages with our parents, we will probably get more of what we want and avoid a lot of arguments and fights!*

The following are examples of what we might say in an "I" message as compared to a bad "YOU" message.

GOOD "I" MESSAGE	BAD "YOU" MESSAGE
"I" am feeling angry.	YOU make me mad.
"I" feel I'm being treated unfairly.	YOU don't treat me fairly.
"I" need to go out at night so I can be with my friends.	YOU never let me go out at night or let me be with anyone.
"I" need a car so I can get around.	YOU don't let me use your car.

"I" feel confined by too many rules.

YOU are too strict with me

"I" feel there are too many demands being put on me.

YOU are too demanding.

"I" feel like there are favorites in our family.

YOU treat (a brother or sister) better than you treat me.

"I" have a problem because I need more spending money.

YOU don't give me enough money.

"I" feel something is always being forced upon me.

YOU always make me do something I don't want to do.

WARNING: "I don't feel **YOU** are treating me fairly" is an example of a camouflaged YOU attack.

To further get this idea across, here are some bad "YOU" messages that our parents use:

YOU don't do this.

YOU don't do that.

YOU are always. . .

YOU need to be more. . .

YOU never. . .

YOU are too. . .

Why can't **YOU**. . .

YOU are so. . .

YOU. . .YOU. . .YOU. . .

Are any of these familiar? I have heard all of them and they really tick me off! Even when my parents are correct in their evaluation, they don't have to be so rude and insensitive. We should try not to treat them this way either.

Do you get the idea of "I" messages? If not, go back and re-read the list of "I" messages and the corresponding "YOU" messages. It is very important that you truly understand this section!

Notice how in an "I" message, we do NOT directly attack our listener, but considerately tell them **how we feel.** Instead of being put on the defensive and/or possibly attacking us in return, the listener will be more inclined to ask how they can help!

Imagine that! We might actually get what we want without getting in a fight! Before the next twenty-four hours are over, I dare you to use an "I" message, for if you do it properly, you will be shocked by the results!

Holy Mackerel! It's time for another pop quiz!

You want to spend some quality time with your Dad. Tell him:
A. YOU never spend any time with me.
B. YOU are never around for me when I need you.
C. Why don't YOU spend more time with me?
D. "I" feel we don't get to spend enough time together and we both are really missing out.

You want your Mom to take you to the store. Tell her:
A. YOU never do anything for me.
B. YOU never take me to the store.
C. Why won't YOU ever take me to the store?
D. Take me to the record store. NOW!
E. I would really like to go to the store. Would you please take me?

Your Mom just said something that is totally unnecessary and really annoying. You should:
A. Attack her with your own comment.
B. Get defensive.
C. Get even by either saying or doing something that really pisses her off.
D. Ignore her pathetic comment with "the silent kiss off" and don't give her the satisfaction of a response.
E. Use an "I" message like, "Mom, my feelings get hurt when I hear comments like that."
F. D and E above.

The following questions relate to how "I" messages help alleviate ambiguity in what we communicate to others.

Because you are very hungry and want to eat **NOW,** you should ask your mother:
A. Is dinner ready?
B. Are we going to eat soon?
C. Why can't we eat earlier?
D. You never have dinner ready when I want to eat.
E. I am so hungry. May I eat now?

Because you want to spend time with a friend and want to eat **LATER,** you should ask your mother:
  A. Is dinner ready?
  B. Are we going to eat soon?
  C. Why can't we eat later?
  D. You never have dinner ready when I want to eat.
  E. I want to go over to a friend's house. May I eat
       dinner later?

Just as a reminder, the best possible answer is the last letter option.

Communicating With Body Language

Remember what body language is? Well, it can also be used to help get a point across. How is your body positioned when talking to a rent or a friend? Is your body slouched, are you walking around swinging your arms in the air like a maniac, are you pointing a finger in an evil way, or shaking a fist? All of these actions give off bad vibes as well as make the listener pay more attention to your actions than to what you are saying. *Would you shake your fist at someone while telling them that you like them???*

When you speak, what is your facial expression? Are you smiling, frowning, crying or laughing? Are your eyes open or closed?

Eyes are an important tool to use when communicating. While talking to a person or group, look everyone in the eye to help emphasize your point. If you look at the ceiling or floor instead, you will make a weak impression. Maintain eye contact so that everyone knows you mean business.

Here is an example of the power of eye contact:
In my freshman year at Penn, two friends and I decided to spend the afternoon in the city. On this day, I

made a horrible mistake which I will never repeat. While riding on the subway to our destination, I made the terrible error of looking directly into the eyes of this huge (and I do mean HUGE!) guy, without quickly looking away.

After a fifteen-second stare down which he obviously won, I immediately asked my friends a question so that this human mountain would see that I was not alone. Then, like a total idiot, I looked back at him and we locked eyes again! This time it lasted about forty-five seconds (and let me tell you, it felt like an eternity!) until my friends saw what was happening and asked me a question of their own. Unfortunately, it was too late. The train had stopped and this guy got up, and kept getting up. He was even bigger than I had imagined. Worst of all, he started to walk slowly toward me!

I couldn't think or move, and if my body had not been frozen in absolute shock, I would have soiled my underwear! Looking up at him in total fear, he leaned over me and whispered, "Looking at people can get you hurt!" Sliding down in my seat, I squeaked, "Okay".

He then turned and left the train.

Often I wonder how I could have been so stupid. Quite frankly, I also wonder why they call Philadelphia the "City of Brotherly Love."

Controlling Our Tone Of Voice

The way in which we express ourselves or pronounce words also plays an important role in getting our ideas and feelings across.

When speaking, what is our tone of voice? Are we speaking sarcastically, belligerently or loudly? What is the tone of our words and how do they sound? Are they uncaring and unfeeling, cold, selfish, accusatory, full of guilt, hard, or insulting? Any of these attitudes paints a negative picture for any person listening to us and even more so for rents! We need to be careful NOT to speak this way!

When speaking, stay cool and collected. Try not to lose your temper, for whenever we lose it, we lose control of the situation. *Repeat that last sentence and try to picture its significance. When I am about to lose my temper, I use slow deep breaths to help calm me down and at the same time, I count to ten (if I'm really angry, I count to a higher number). This often prevents me from putting my foot in my mouth and size 12C is not a very comfortable fit! Sometimes, I even excuse myself from the conversation and just walk away.*

There is one thing for sure, temper tantrums are self-destructive. This brings to mind a fortune I once got from a fortune cookie: "Anger begins with folly and ends in regret."

This is the last section of this chapter so keep on truckin'.

Poor Communication

Remember, poor communication either does not properly express to the listener what we want them to understand, or is communication that can be taken negatively. In short, avoid poor communication!

Now let's go over some examples of the "not too good" things we say to our parents in stead of our true feelings.

1. We should be careful what we call our parents. Do **NOT** call parents *those wonderful names like* mean, uncaring, unthoughtful, unloving, inconsiderate, unfair, jerks, stupid, assholes, *to name a few,* for they might think that as long as you feel this way, they should live up to your expectations. This tactic of attacking the speaker rather than the speaker's ideas, backfires on us, just as it backfires on the rents when they call us bad names like spoiled, lazy, untrustworthy, irresponsible... to try to get us to act and do what they want. *Not that I have ever been called any of these names!* Most importantly, comments which attack character are never appreciated, may harm our relationship, and hurt feelings.

2. Just as we hate when our parents say things like, "why can't you be more like (so and so)?" or "Why

can't you be more grown up?" our parents dislike certain comments that we use all too quickly. Here are a few:

"Why can't you be like (a friend's) mom/dad?" The

Why can't you be like Weasel's mom? SHE rents us dirty movies and buys us popcorn !!

only logical answer is the same answer you gave when you were asked the same thing, "Because I'm not (your friend's) mom/dad." "I didn't ask to be born" is another comment parents don't like. After all, who actually asks to be born? *I would love to know who first thought of such a profound question!*

3. The vague, *"Up yours, you do not matter,"* answers we give our parents are a definite "NO NO." Here are some more examples of ambiguous responses:

Question:	Answer:
"What did you do this afternoon?"	"Nothing" or "Nothing much."
"Where did you go?"	"Out."
"Why did you do that?"	"Because" *(or for some smart asses,"Why not?")*

These are bad responses, because they make a parent feel that we don't care enough to share a part of our life with them. They also imply that we are purposely hiding something. What we should do is "throw them a crumb" by telling them some tiny insignificant fact. *Please know that I'm not suggesting you tell them that on your date last night, you ended up in a motel with a wonderful vibrating water bed.* However, do tell them a little of what happened.

But, if you really are very close to your parents and can get them to promise not to punish you or make any negative comments, tell them about the motel. After all, your rents are not virgins, but are humans who have been around the block a couple of thousand times them-

selves! They might even know about the crack in the mirror above the bed in the room you visited! By sharing with them some of your experiences or thoughts, they may just surprise you and tell you some of their own.

Most importantly, parents really appreciate our openness and friendship. After all, if we want our parents to be friends, we have

57

to treat them like friends.

4. Bad communication does not even have to be spoken aloud to be bad. Being flippant by mouthing words or mimicking rents can really piss them off!

A prank which you can play on your parents is the gibberish game. My father is a perfect candidate for this trick, as he is a little hard of hearing. Here's what to do: When there are people around and it is noisy, I look at my father and say something like the following, "Boy this tred blod dree crat yellow, but kred srap carto rado grad. Boy it was unbelievable!"

Well, as you have just tried to read, most of this sentence makes absolutely no sense at all. My father, in trying to understand what I have just told him, will make me repeat it over and over until he catches on, or I start laughing.

It's okay to be a little obnoxious, just don't overdo it!

5. Using **sarcasm** or any emotionally **painful jokes** in which a parent is made to look like a fool *(which they probably are)* is poor communication. When a parent becomes the victim of this slanderous method of expression, they will get even, and in the end, everyone gets hurt.

6. **ASK**, do not demand. Just as we are usually polite with our friends in asking for a favor, try to do the same with parents. A "demand" by us will give them a reason **NOT** to give us what we want.

7. I hate to be **judged, blamed,** or **accused,** and truly believe most people feel the same way. With this in mind, we should not judge, blame, or accuse our parents, especially when they are in public or in a bad frame of mind.

and finally the best for last...

8. Sometimes, the worst communication on our part is any communication at all. *Occasionally, it is best just to keep our traps closed and not use our "freedom of speech."* For example, when a parent says something that is absolutely ridiculous or insulting, it is better to respond by **NOT** responding. By doing this, it shows them that we are not going to get into a fight or give them the satisfaction of a response. *This is another aspect of the "Silent Kiss Off."*

Chapter 7: Tools and Techniques
For Better Communication

Using Questions To Communicate

Questions are one of the greatest tools available to use against anyone, especially parents. The key to any question is the manner in which it is asked, for if worded properly, a question can be deadly!

But why are questions so important to us kids when dealing with parents? The answer is this: **Rarely can we get into trouble by asking a legitimate and honest question as long as we ask it in an innocent and sincere way.** Furthermore, mature and responsible adults, like parents and teachers, can usually be forced to answer any reasonable question.

For example: *In my last year of math in high school, our teacher attempted to teach us calculus. I had no idea why we would ever want to take first derivatives of functions, so one day, I finally asked our teacher why we were doing this and how it would help us later in life. Everyone in the class laughed and she tried to pass the question off as a joke.*

I became very serious and kept my ground by asking the question again, but in an even more sincere way. She had no choice but to answer the question and spent the rest of the class trying to come up with different ways we might take first derivatives of functions later in life. An entire class was wasted and everyone had a great time watching our teacher scramble!

To this day, the only time that I have ever thought

about taking the first derivative of a function is to come up with a system to help my grandfather handicap horses. Well, I guess our calculus teacher was correct, one can use calculus later in life. It all goes to show you that a high school education can really come in handy!

Purposes of Communicating With Questions

1. Questions are obviously best used for "Probing." By using the example of your parents playing golf instead of lending you the car (in chapter one), you can get them to confess or let them know that you are aware of their deception by just using questions. For example, at the dinner table that night, ask your mom/dad how your grandmother is feeling. Do not ask any questions to which they can answer "yes" or "no," since you want to make them give their own explanation.

2. By using questions, accusations can be made in an innocent way. *Pretty handy!* If someone confronts you and suggests that your question is an implication, respond innocently that you have no idea what they are talking about. You have not implied anything, but have simply asked a question. You can even go a step further by asking them why they are acting paranoid!

Using the same example, if your father responds, "are you trying to tell me that you don't think we went to grandma's?" or "are you implying something?" Your reply to your father could be, "I didn't say that. Did you hear me say that?" He will have to say "no." Remember, answer all his questions with a question until he gives a real answer.

This same type of accusing question can border on slander. An illustration is the following: Two politicians are running against each other for the same office. The race becomes very heated and they start to insult each other. One candidate asks the other, "How often did you steal from the treasury in your last term of office?" Even without any response, this question implies that he has stolen from the treasury.

3. Answering a question with a question is an excellent method of evading any question.

Changing The Subject

Changing the subject of a conversation can be enormously useful. It can be done with your friends or parents when they are talking about something you don't want to discuss. If done subtly, no one is the wiser.

To successfully change the subject of a conversation, ignore what is being said and pick an entirely different subject matter to discuss. This new topic of discussion must be interesting to everyone so they will forget the original subject.

To illustrate: *It is Saturday morning and Mom, Dad and I are eating breakfast. The subject of conversation turns to what I did last night. If for any reason, I don't want to share what happened, I might look out the window at my Mom's garden, and ask Dad with Mom hearing the question, "Don't you think a rock garden would look good in that area of the yard instead of Mom's flowers?"*

Although Dad might consider the question for the moment, to insure that he doesn't touch her garden, my panicking Mom will quickly respond before he even has a chance to open his mouth. (My Mom loves to garden, although she has a tough time keeping any plant other than a cactus or weed alive for any period longer than a month. The local nurseries just adore her!) At this point, he will either agree with me to tease my mother, or he will think I'm crazy for asking.

It doesn't matter. Mom has forgotten about the original question and is thinking of her precious flowers. I will then change the subject again to what my father thinks the New Orleans Saints will do on Sunday, a topic of great interest for Dad. It usually takes two changes before the initial topic is forgotten. They have such poor concentration, it sometimes amazes me.

The best and most successful "change of subject" is posing a question that is subtle and interesting to everyone in the conversation. **You should also be aware when someone, especially a parent, changes the subject on you!**

Multiple Choice:

A friend asks you, in front of a lot of people, something you find embarrassing or sensitive. Answer them by saying:
   A. Why are you asking me this question?
   B. What concern is it of yours?
   C. Ignore the question.
   D. Pose a sensitive and embarrassing question of your own to them and do not stop asking yours until they stop asking theirs.
   E. Any of the above.

That's all for this chapter. Get ready for the next chapter, as it should give you some ideas to help increase your allowance. . .

Chapter 8: Everything is a Negotiation

Have you ever heard of the book, The Art of War, by Sun Tzu? It was written by a Chinese general thousands of years ago and it is fantastic. Well, what you are about to read is my "Art of Negotiating," and although it may not be as ancient, it should be very helpful in adding to your new abilities to manage parents.

I parallel the Art of Negotiating to The Art of War because a negotiation is a type of "battle." If you go into a negotiation unprepared without the appropriate "weapons," or the "desire to win," then just like in war, you will lose.

Now, let me ask you a few questions: Do you think that you will ever rent an apartment? buy a car? build a house? hire someone to work for you? ask a friend for a big favor? or ask a parent for money or a new privilege? If you plan to do any of the above, you will in some manner need to use your negotiating skills.

*In fact, even if you're not aware of it, practically every time you have dealt with parents or any other person, a negotiation has taken place. You just have never thought of it that way. When confronting someone face to face in order to change or influence their opinions or values, you are negotiating. As you probably know, it is not the actual negotiation that counts, but the **end results!***

By the way, congratulations! You have reached the "official half way point."

Truly successful negotiations have an outcome that is fair because all parties agree to the final terms. If a negotiation has not gone well, either you were not in a good position to negotiate, you negotiated poorly, and/or your opponent feels the same way that you feel since it also went poorly for them.

When dealing with parents, never allow a win/lose scenario (when either party feels as if they have lost from the negotiation), for it leads to bad feelings and communication breakdown. **Everyone should win if possible.** Don't forget, we don't want to hurt our parents or make them **feel** as if we have taken advantage of them.

The Art Of Negotiating

The following ideas apply to more than just parents, but the word "parents" or "rents" will be substituted for any opposing party. *Fitting huh? Because I feel that this topic is very important to managing parents, I have intentionally kept the tone serious.*

1. Necessities for the negotiation:

A. Do your parents have something that you want (the use of a car, a larger allowance, more privileges, etc.)?

B. Do you have something that your parents want or that you can induce them to want (good grades, a clean room, etc.)?

C. Are you in a position to negotiate? Do your parents have any reason to listen to you? Can you afford to walk away from the negotiations? Do you have other alternatives? If so, you are in a good position. If you cannot walk away from the negotiating table, then your parents will have the upper hand unless they are in the same position as you. *Let's face facts, our parents can't walk away from the negotiating table any more than we can, although they pretend they can. It's called ing," so don't be fooled.*

2. Preparation for the negotiation:

A. Always try to **make a plan** before confronting parents. Some sayings which reflect this idea are: "plan your work and work your plan" and "the man with the plan will reap from the land." Planning is paramount to any successful negotiation and the best planning is done on paper, since your thoughts can actually be visualized.

B. Figure out exactly what you want from your rents and list these objectives according to importance. *Negotiating is pretty tough if you don't know what you want.* For example, you got the car for the evening, but it doesn't have any gas. The negotiation should have been for the car and some gas money. Set parameters and facilitate your negotiation by knowing the best possible result(s) and bare minimum result(s) that are acceptable to you.

C. **Anticipate** what your parent's reactions and demands will be. Remember, few things are free, and parents will probably want something out of the deal now or later. *That's just the way things are. Moreover, if you are not willing to give up anything during the negotiation,* **everyone** *may lose. I believe this is a horrible outcome, for I don't believe in losing!*

Look to past events and negotiations to determine what parents typically want from you. *You will get better at this since rents are pretty consistent. Eventually, predicting what rents want will become second nature.*

Evaluate your parents' needs and feelings (look back to the answers in chapter 4). Know what you are willing to give into (called concessions). Decide what you will not give into (called deal breakers).

D. **Good timing** is essential to negotiating! When planning strategy, pick the optimum moment to approach your parent(s). Obviously, the best time is when parents are in good moods. For example, *When my Dad comes home from work, he is tired, uptight, and always hungry. To ask him for anything at this time is clearly bad timing. It is far better to wait about an hour after dinner to deal with him. At this time in the evening, he is about as tame as he gets, except of course when he is asleep.*

DAD, can I get a Harley? ...Does that mean "yes?" Huh Dad? Huh?

Another example of "bad timing" is trying to discuss a subject with parents when they are pressed for time. It doesn't allow us the time to express our thoughts and when rents have to make quick judgements, unless it is something they have already agreed to in the past, their decision usually goes against us.

Remember, parents are not computers. What they are **feeling** at any given moment will strongly determine what we receive from the negotiation.

E. Always try to pick the best **location** where the advantage is yours, or at least a spot that is fair to you.

Whenever possible, do not negotiate in your paren-

67

t's room, as this is on their turf and you will be at a disadvantage. Try to negotiate in your room, the kitchen, the dining room or the living room.

An example of how adults use location against us is the following: *In lower school, my teacher saw me chewing gum in the class room and said to me, "I told you that there is no chewing gum in class. Please throw away your gum." With all my friends and classmates watching, I had fun throwing my gum away by making a big production of walking to the trash can and placing the gum inside. My classmates had a good laugh and I won by getting some attention.*

The next time the teacher caught me chewing gum, she picked a neutral place where I could not make a "scene" out of throwing my gum away; she asked me to  *come with her outside of the room, into the hallway. She then told me the same thing, "I told you that there is no chewing gum in class. Please throw away your gum." I was now dealing with her one-on-one and she had the advantage. After putting my tail between my legs, I complied immediately with her wishes.*

The last time she caught me chewing gum, she decided to teach me a lesson and asked me to follow her out of the room. She lead me to the principal's office where in front of the entire administrative staff she stated the same exact thing to me, "I told you that there is no chewing gum in class. Please throw away your gum." In *this location, I was so intimidated that I swallowed my gum! To this day, I hate gum.*

In each scene, the message and the teacher were identical, but the location varied. As a result, my response changed with each location.

Never attempt to negotiate with parents in public or where others can overhear the discussion. In public, parents fear that they might lose face by appearing to have no discipline or control over their children -- us. *The moral is: always show extra respect around parents when in public, even if they do not deserve it.* If they are not alone and you must talk to them about something serious, ask to see them in private.

Also, negotiations on any serious matter should not be attempted on the phone, but face to face. Because it is more difficult for parents to say "no" while looking you in the eyes, dealing with parents in person is more effective. In essence, a telephone is a very impersonal method of communication (with parents or friends) and shouldn't be used when trying to negotiate.

F. Always bring a pen and pad of paper to the negotiation so that you can take notes. In doing this, your notes will prevent you from forgetting important points that you want to make. Furthermore, by writing notes, you won't have to interrupt your parent for fear of forgetting a rebuttal. *The best part is that your parents will be surprised by your pen and pad, but will know that you are taking the discussion very seriously and will therefore take you more seriously!*

G. Although it is not always possible, try to **negotiate with one parent at a time.** Always pick the parent who you think will give the best response. At the proper time and when he or she is alone, confront them and sell them on your idea. This is helpful, for when parents are together negotiating against you, they can gang up against you or do a tag team. This is where one parent argues and lets the other watch and prepare another argument until they have blasted you so much that you will wish you had just simply asked to be grounded.

Together, parents can also act as a pair of judges, instead of negotiators. When this happens, you won't even get to state your point of view, for they have already judged you and will not listen to what you have to say. Finally, when dealing with two parents, you have to fulfill both parents' desires in order to get what you want.

All I can say is that negotiating with both parents is a very disturbing experience, because you can easily lose control of the situation. Don't let one rent tell you, "Let's wait until the other parent gets home before we discuss this matter." If you do, you will probably be put at a great disadvantage.

Like other military strategists, my belief is "divide and conquer." *Besides, it's just too easy to attack one parent at a time.* Get one parent on your side and then go after the other. This is the best possible tactic, as parents usually depend upon each other for strength. *I just love it when my Dad tells me, "If your mother says it's all right, it's okay with me." Fortunately, Mom has already said the same thing about Dad, so the problem in question is solved!*

Just about everyone has played one parent against the other, but doing so is bad. For example, your mother says "no" to something that you want, so you go to your father. If either parent finds out what you have done, it will be "big trouble," as they both can lose trust in you. This is a risk you should **not** take.

I'm not suggesting that you should give up. Instead,

the best technique is to go to your dad, but make sure to tell him, up front, what your mom's feelings are.

3. The proper attitudes for the negotiation:

A. Although it is sometimes difficult, have **patience** when dealing with parents. Besides, sometimes the person you are negotiating with is pressed to finish the negotiation quickly, so by stalling a little, they will give you more concessions in order to close the deal faster. Be patient!

B. **Keep calm and cool** when negotiating. Do not lose your temper or parents will focus their attention on your emotional outburst and not on your argument, *and then you are really in trouble.* Any kind of emotional display is destructive to your position. *Act* courteous and respectful. *Do you like it when they scream at you?* Instead of speaking louder when upset, try whispering. It's ten times more effective. Try it!

C. **Be open-minded.** Listen carefully to your parents' views (active listening). It is critical to interpret the true meaning of what they are saying. By doing this, you can avoid unnecessary confusion and have better and quicker results from the discussion. Most importantly, you can often catch flaws in their argument and use them to your advantage!

4. Helpful hints for the successful negotiation:

A. Come to the discussion with a preconceived, but flexible strategy. After hearing what your parents say, you might need to change your strategy.

B. Try to let your parents state their demands first. When they do this, you learn about their position and can start to discuss their demands without any guess work. Now since you know exactly what they want from you, you will be in a better position to decide on a strategy. This also saves you from making unnecessary concessions that your rents have not considered asking for.

C. Be persistent in defending your position, whatever it may be. Be firm and don't give in to parents too quickly. If too many concessions are made too soon, you will have nothing to negotiate with later.

D. Don't rush yourself. Talk slowly so that you can think clearly and formulate your ideas! If you have to pause to gather your thoughts, don't worry, this is a natural part of negotiating. *In fact, if parents had their way, we would have absolutely no time to think about our strategy and they would keep us totally confused and on the defensive.* Take your time and tell them how you appreciate their patience.

E. Be truthful and convincing. Believe in what you say and use controlled emotions to emphasize important points. Sell yourself and your point of view with convincing phrasing so that they will **want** to help. (Use "I" statements)

F. Don't be afraid to ask for anything. Everything is negotiable; it is only the price that needs to be established. If they say that some of your demands are not up for discussion, ask them why. When they explain their reasoning, ask if there is any middle-ground. Keep after them.

G. Build a "straw man" during your negotiations by acting as if something is really important to you when it is not. When you finally give in to their demands and give up your "straw man," your parents will feel as if they have won a major victory (when in fact they have not). As a result, your position improves, for they will now believe they owe you something.

H. Do not be afraid to **respectfully** say "NO" ("Mom/Dad, with all due **respect,** NO.") or that you **respectfully** disagree with something that your parents have said. ("Sorry, but I respectfully disagree.") This is a part of negotiating, and although your parents may think that you are being flippant, they must be convinced that you have heard what they said, but that you honestly do not agree with their **point of view.** Do not attack them personally, but deal only with the issues.

I. Never tell the rents that you will "consider something," because this is making a concession. They will take for granted that if you will consider something, you will ultimately do it! On the contrary, try to get your parents to tell you that they will at least consider your request!

J. In negotiating with parents, not all questions need to be answered. Some questions that parents ask do NOT deserve an answer. *Do they tell us **everything?** If you think they do, you are probably very mistaken!* When uncomfortable questions come up, try to evade them by asking a question of your own in return.

If you want to learn how to evade questions, just watch presidential debates. You will see how candidates can speak for several minutes without saying anything in response to a question posed to them. *It's just amazing and pathetic!*

Should your parents keep pushing, use the **truth.** *The truth is a great tool!* Diplomatically say, "I'm sorry, but that question is too personal to answer," or "I'm sorry, but I simply don't feel comfortable answering that question."

K. Silence or a pause in the conversation can be an powerful tool when negotiating. Silence can be used to make someone feel uneasy or to force them to make the next move in a conversation. The easiest way to create this unnatural pause in the conversation, as well as to determine the period of silence, is to count to yourself (counting to seven is usually sufficient).

L. In any conversation, if you really want to get someone's attention, touch them. This simple action also helps get your point across. (I have found that the best way to touch someone is to casually extend my hand in a natural way and simply touch or even gently pinch their arm.) You will be amazed how well this simple invasion of their body space works.

M. Don't get bogged down on a little topic, but keep your attention on the big picture. Furthermore, when giving into a parent's demand, make it contingent upon your receiving something in return. This way, everyone will benefit.

N. Knowledge and information are indispensable when negotiating. If you know something that your parents don't, use it. *After all, turn-about is fair play, as our parents do the same to us.*

O. After you finally succeed in getting what you want and the deal is closed, either talk about something else, or thank them and leave the room. Don't keep discussing the issue as they may change their minds. *Please re-read this paragraph. I have screwed up by not following this idea.*

P. Don't attack your parent's position "as a parent" by stating anything like: "I will do as I want." "You can't make me." "You can't tell me what to do." "I don't care." "I don't care what you think." *Comments like these will only piss off a parent even worse and you'll never win your point.*

Q. If possible, get your brothers or sisters to support you. This is helpful because there is strength in numbers.

R. A good place to get ideas and advice for problems that arise with your parents is from an older brother or sister. If you're the oldest kid in the family, you will be paving the way for younger brother(s) and sister(s).

S. Always evaluate past negotiations with rents to see if any improvements can be made for future negotiations. This analysis helps, as each negotiation, whether successful or not, should be used as a learning experience.

Every negotiation has five potential results: **1) Both YOU and your PARENTS WIN;** 2) You win and your parents lose; 3) Your parents win and you lose; 4) Both you and your parents lose; 5) Nothing happens as no agreement is reached.

Since the object of negotiating is to work through problems to find an acceptable solution that fulfills **everyone's needs,** your goal should always be for **Both You and your Parents to WIN**. The perfect end to a negotiation is one in which everyone is happy. If there are any bad feelings, these bad feelings can damage future dealings *and everyone ultimately loses when this happens!*

Since your parents have much more experience than you, initially they will be better negotiators. In fact, on your first couple of confrontations, you will walk away shaking your head wondering,"what happened?" Don't let a couple of losses discourage you. These bruises do heal.

No one can win every time. Just make sure that

you pick your battles carefully (know when it is prudent to back off) so that you don't win the battle and lose the war.

Finally, the momentous day will come when you will "kick butt" and your parents will walk away shaking their heads, wondering what happened, *while you*

laugh yourself silly. Eventually, both sides will be able to negotiate so that everyone wins or at least perceives that they have won.

Asking Parents For Money $$$

Allow me to demonstrate some of these negotiating ideas at work. The following example: **Asking parents for money $$$,** will also introduce you to other managerial tools, *as well as some hints to raise your allowance!*

Hitting parents up for money is a task I have always hated. There was this ever-present feeling of helplessness of being at their total mercy. After a little practice, and watching my sister at work (she was a pro), I too became

76

proficient. To get the job done, consider heeding the following suggestions:

Be Appreciative: Always thank both parents for any money that either one of them gives you. They

work hard for their money and appreciation by you is, to say the least, appropriate. Furthermore, they will be more likely to give you money in the future if they know that you truly appreciate what you receive.

Respect Your Parents' Money: *Every parent loves to remind us that money doesn't grow on trees. Even though I hate that cliche, parents are obviously correct by pointing out that money must be earned with hard work.* With this in mind, don't ask for money all the time. If you do, they will feel that you are squandering their hard earned cash, that you are a spendthrift, or that you are possibly even abusing them. Avoid making them feel this way at all costs.
Live with the money that they give you or try to negotiate for a little more to prevent repetitive requests for more money. Every now and then, when given money,

let your parents know how much you respect their money by telling them that you don't need so much and offer some of it back to them. Don't worry, they will rarely take any back. This is one of the greatest ploys for future increases. Also, by doing this, they get the message that you are not going to needlessly spend their money and that you respect the hard work it required to earn it. *Besides, you get to see a confused look on their faces.*

Location: Any location is acceptable to ask a parent for money, as long as it is done **tactfully.** This is even true when your parents are with their friends, because they just love to show how generous they are with their children. *You will quickly learn to cherish this attribute of generosity in public.*

There are three components to a public request for money:

1) Whisper the request to your parent so that they don't lose face if they don't have enough money to give you. If they do have extra cash to give, they can make a big display of their generosity.

2) When they give you money (no matter how much they have given you), tell them in front of their friends that you don't need so much and offer to give **some** of it back. Don't worry, they will always refuse your offer because they will want to look generous.

This publicly demonstrates to your parents' friends how you value their money, something that their own kids probably do not do. *So what if the other kids get hell from their rents when they get home; that's their problem.*

3) After they give you money in public, continuously thank them *until you start feeling nauseous.* This shows that you are really appreciative and well brought up.

Timing: Timing is very important to guarantee that you receive money from your parents. Know when your rent is in a good mood. *As I have said, I would never ask my father for money before dinner!* Furthermore, it is easier to make a case for yourself in front of one parent, since you only have to satisfy one parent's needs.

Discover when your parents' paydays are. When their wallets are full, they tend to be a little more liberal with their funds! Learn whether they are paid weekly, every other week, or monthly and on what day (usually on a Friday).

If possible, try not to ask for any money when they are short of funds, for this is just **bad timing.** The truth of the matter is that every time we ask for money and it is refused, parents feel badly and have regrets. It is our fault for not having better prepared the assault on their wallets.

Amusement: Amuse your parents so that they enjoy giving you money. Tell them how you are going to spend their money and what you will do with what you buy. You have to sell your parents on whatever it is that you wish to purchase by showing them that you know a lot about the purchase. In doing this, they will see how important it is to you.

As we get older, it is more and more important to let our parents know what we do with the money they give us. If we tell a fun and interesting story regarding what we plan to do or have done with their money, they become happier and more inclined to give us more money in the future. *It's called a "snow job"-- I mean "sell job."*

Living Vicariously: Let your parents give you advice and information on what you wish to purchase. In doing this, vicariously, they are buying what you are buying. *As far as I'm concerned, they can live this way as long as I get the buck$!* To illustrate: *I wanted to purchase a suit for college, but didn't know if my rents would go for the idea. By asking them to help me to pick out the style, color, weight of the cloth, etc., (I really didn't know what I wanted anyway) they were more than happy to buy the suit since they were buying what they would want to wear and were happy doing so. It sure is fun keeping them happy!*

Helpful Hint: When parents agree to reimburse us for something we buy, always give them the receipt for the purchase. Parents like this show of honesty!

By following these ideas, the next time you ask for money, not only will your parents be more likely to open up their wallets, they might open them wider. If, however, you cannot convince them to pry open their wallets, don't fret or make a big scene. Think positive -- you'll get them next time!

Multiple Choice:

In any negotiation, the purpose is to:
  A. Let the person we are negotiating with take advantage of us.
  B. Beat the hell out of the opposing party and take them for everything we can.
  C. Make it so no one wins.
  D. Make sure we get what we want, yet leave something on the table for the other party so that they feel like winners too.

Before negotiating with a parent, always:
  A. Make a plan.
  B. Determine what you want and what you will give
     to get what you want.
  C. Determine which parent you wish to approach.
  D. Determine the best time to approach them.
  E. All of the above.

The best time to negotiate with your parents is:
  A. After your mom has totalled the car in an accident.
  B. After your dad has told you that he has lost his job.
  C. After your parents have just had a gut wrenching
     fight with each other.
  D. All of the above.
  E. When a parent is happy, calm, cool (not rushed)
     and feels great about the world.

The best location to confront your parents for a negotiation is:
  A. Where your parents are easily embarrassed.
  B. Where your parents can easily lose face.
  C. Where your parents are rushed.
  D. In their room.
  E. At a private location where your parents do not
     have an advantage, and where everyone is
     relaxed and at ease.

When you are negotiating:
  A. Scream at them until they give you what you want.
  B. Get personal and insult your parents so they give
     you what you want.
  C. Have a temper tantrum and demand what you
     deserve.
  D. All of the above.
  E. Be patient, keep calm, cool, and use "I" messages
     and active listening.

After you get what you want from your parents:
  A. Say and do nothing.
  B. Laugh in their face and scream,"A fool is born
      every day!"
  C. Smile and shoot the bird.
  D. B. and C. above.
  E. Thank them and then change the subject or thank
      them and leave them alone before they change
      their minds.

Your mom thinks you are driving to your friend's house,
but you are really headed to the convenience store. She
asks you, "on your way home, please get me a gallon of
milk." Answer her:
  A. No.
  B. Get your own milk.
  C. Use your own milk, you big old cow!
  D. Build a straw man by telling her, "I am doing this
      favor for you even though it is out of my way
      (not in the same food isle) because you are such
      a wonderful mother."

When we want money from our parents, we should:
  A. Pick their pockets when they are not looking.
  B. Take them to the cleaners.
  C. Take them to the cleaners and leave them there.
  D. Hold them upside down when they are not looking
      and shake real hard. Hopefully some money
      will fall out of their "tight pockets!"
  E. Politely ask for money and then make them feel
      good about giving us the funds by thanking them
      and telling them how much we appreciate their
      generosity.

Again, the best answer to each multiple choice question is the last letter option.

Answer the following True or False:

When negotiating:
1. Let your parents state their demands first.
2. Don't cave into their demands too easily.
3. Take your time and think things through.
4. Sell your ideas to them.
5. Don't be afraid to ask for anything.
6. Try to make your parents feel like they have won some issue that is important to them so that they now owe you something.
7. Do NOT tell your rents that you will consider something, but try to get them to tell you what they will consider doing for you.
8. When necessary, use silence to make them make the next move.
9. Don't get bogged down on a little topic and lose sight of the big picture, or your ultimate goal.
10. When you get what you want, close the discussion and go on to other topics.

The best answer to all the above questions is True. If you feel an answer was more appropriately answered false, please re-read part 5, Helpful Hints to Successful Negotiations, and reconsider.

Chapter 9: Managing Our Parents

At last -- you've done it! You have persevered through the first eight chapters to get to the moment for which you have been waiting. Haven't you? If you have skipped any chapters, may the flies of a thousand camels infest your armpits.

This chapter is the voyage of no return, the final plunge to managing your parents! There's no looking back, but only forward to controlling your own destiny. Congratulations!

Hold your breath now as I define what managing parent(s) is:

any action on your part that influences their values such that their response fulfills your need(s).

For you readers who are like me and are not exactly rocket scientists, here is a simpler version: you can manage someone by **1) changing their values so that their new values will make them do something you desire; or 2) using some action to influence their present values so that they will fulfill your needs.** *If you've forgotten, you can breathe now!*

Changing a parent's values or beliefs is the first method for management. It is a simple and useful tactic *that, unfortunately, is not fully taken advantage of by us. You see, rents do the crazy, abnormal, and wondrously obnoxious things that they do because their values and beliefs dictate their actions.* These values and beliefs are

84

determined by their upbringing, their religious beliefs, their moral values (or lack there of), and the many lifetime experiences that they have encountered during the centuries that they have lived.

An example of changing a parent's beliefs is illustrated in Chapter 2 when I changed my Mom's values and beliefs so that she would not punish me when I told the truth. Mom valued hearing the truth about what was happening in my life more than her ability to punish me. The following is another illustration.

We were having a typical family dinner at home with everyone sitting around the kitchen table eating a "well balanced meal" when all of a sudden, my Mom reached over into my plate and stole some of my food. No matter how much I had ever complained or bitched at her about taking my food, it was the same old thing; she would still grab a partially eaten chicken bone, cob of corn or just some random scrap that she thought I had finished eating. This was so aggravating! After all, what was on my plate was mine, no matter whether I still wanted to eat it or not.

Discouraging Mom from her habit of eating my food was an impossibility, or was it? Well, a revelation struck me one evening. We were eating dinner and Mom was being her usual self by stealing my food. I had had enough!

I took a string-bean off of my plate and called the dog over to my side of the table. Our dog at the time was a twelve-year-old graying dachshund with half of its teeth missing. The dog didn't miss any of his teeth anyway as its voracious appetite hindered any chewing of its food.

The four legged land shark, seeing a scrap of food fall to the floor, pounced. After a quick smell and a gum-

ming of the morsel that had fallen, the dog realized that I was trying to trick it into eating a string-bean with some gravy for covering. (smart dog huh?!?)

I pointed to the partially chewed string-bean on the floor and showed Mom that the little beast still didn't like string-beans. She laughed and told me to clean up the mess I had made. (The dog had really made most of the mess, but this was a losing argument, so I didn't pursue it.) I picked up the string-bean, put it back on my plate (away from all of the food that I still wanted to eat of course), continued to eat my dinner and waited. . .

Like clockwork, Mom's fork flashed into my food, but this time I said nothing. I glanced down and the mangled string-bean with glistening dog saliva and dirt from the floor was gone. Out of the corner of my eye, I saw Mom put the string bean to her lips and for a brief moment (a very brief moment), felt a tug of allegiance to warn her, but the moment quickly disappeared and so did the string-bean. I watched her chew it and then swallow.

With a grin as wide as the Mississippi River, I asked her if she had enjoyed the string-bean. She smiled and told me that she had. I then informed her of the string-bean's history and started to laugh uncontrollably. Mom just sat there with a sick look on her face making unintelligible sounds.

That was the last time Mom ever

reached into my food without my prior approval to eat from my plate. Since Mom's beliefs about the quality of food in my plate had changed, her actions changed.

Here is a another example of how I caused a slow change in both of my parent's **values** and **beliefs:** *Every weekend in high school, my parents and I had a battle on Friday night over the time I had to be in the house and then fought again on Saturday night. I'm sure you know what I'm talking about! I really began to tire of the weekly fighting and hearing them say, "We are worried about you, not knowing where you are, who you are with, and what you are doing." (Sounds like a little distrust to me, huh!)*

Well, after much thought, I decided to try something new. That next weekend when we were about to have our usual skirmish about my curfew, they repeated in their whining voices almost verbatim, "We are worried about you, not knowing where you are, who you are with, and what you are doing." I asked them if these were their only concerns. They laughed and quickly assured me that this was more than enough to be worried about! Well, I had them. They fell right into my trap!

I then told them that I had an idea which would alleviate their fears and concerns, while allowing me to stay out later. When they skeptically asked me what I had in mind, my response was, "At midnight, I will call you up and tell you where I am, who I am with, and what I am doing."

My words created that look that only a rent can have when they think a fast one is being pulled over them. But after much discussion, we agreed that if they didn't like the outcome, they could go back to the old method without an argument from me. I convinced them to at least try it once. The curfew was set for 1:00 a.m., provided that I called promptly at midnight.

(When you want a new privilege, you can usually get your parents to give you the privilege on a "test basis." That is, if the new privilege is handled "responsibly," the new privilege is yours to keep. *If you screw up, your parents can revoke the privilege without any argument, just as they would anyway!* Every success on your part will help you in the future with obtaining new privileges. The opposite is also true, for every failure will become a stumbling block.)

That night at the stroke of midnight, I put my quarter into the phone and called my rents from our local hangout, a neighborhood bar, and told them the required information. (In New Orleans, the drinking age was 18, so most kids who were old enough to drive, age fifteen (without braces), could get into almost any drinking establishment.)

Surprisingly enough, my parents were satisfied with this new plan. From that night on, every Friday and Saturday night, at twelve sharp, I would call them to "report in," probably disturbing whatever parents do late at night when the kids are out of the house and they are alone. (A sickening thought, I might add.) My curfew of 1:00 A.M. soon turned into 2:00 A.M. and even-

tually disappeared.

*After a couple of years of midnight calls just to tell them that I was still alive, my father finally informed me one morning that except in an emergency, I should stop bothering them late at night. **Their concerns and beliefs had totally changed and I did as I pleased.***

It should be noted that on a couple of occasions, due to having too much fun, I forgot to call them at midnight! Boy, was I in a load of trouble when I got home and Dad was sitting in the living room in his pajamas wearing war paint. To say he was rather "unthrilled" would be a serious understatement!

*Having that distinct feeling that I was in **IT** deep and deserved a whopper of a punishment, I apologized almost fifty times telling him I was sorry and that it would not happen again before he could even open his mouth. I gave no excuse since this would only piss him off even more. (if it was possible!) After a quick chewing of my "derriere," he felt better and ordered me to go to sleep.*

Remember, a parent's values and beliefs won't change overnight. These values and beliefs must be continuously influenced until they have changed enough to fulfill your needs. As always, planning and forethought are necessary to accomplish the change.

Managing people by the second definition, **Influencing Values,** can be done in two ways: the **positive incentive,** or the **negative motivator.** *To get a better picture, try to imagine a carrot (the positive incentive), hanging in front of a donkey pulling a cart, and the driver, you, holding a whip (the negative motivator).*

Most simply stated, characteristics of the carrot are actions, on our part, that will benefit our parents (directly or indirectly), and "positively" motivate them to do what we want. By fulfilling their needs and desires, our parents will feel happier toward us and be more apt to fulfill our needs and desires. *If you think about it, this give and take is only fair.*

The following are some positive motivators:

Enjoy, Amuse, and Love Parents

The time that we spend with our parents should be enjoyable and fun. This includes playing with parents, and amusing them. Although this can be done in many ways, make sure that when amusing them, they are in a receptive mood so that they are amused and not annoyed. *In other words, I would not try to amuse my dad if he were suffering from a bad case of hemorrhoids!*

Share with your parents stories of what is happening to you and your friends and make them sound bigger than life. Reminisce about the good times that you have had together, *even if there are only a handful.*

Humor is a fun and terrific tool to use in managing parents. When we are witty and comical, our parents' amusement will be appreciated *and ultimately rewarded later on.*

Try to make them laugh and play all sorts of ridiculous pranks that touch their funny bones. *Believe it or not, they will relive these events over and over when they are with their friends.* Have playful arguments over the most ridiculous subjects, and let them win. *Be creative!*

Love is an intangible feeling which should always be felt by all parties in a parent/child relationship. *Even when we have been punished, and are putting hexes and curses on our parents, we still love them.* How many people can you honestly say you love? Love is just too precious. It should never be used as a tool for any purpose, by either party.

We should tell our parents that we love them. Saying, "I love you," is so simple and yet, sometimes, so incredibly difficult to say. This is especially true if we rarely ever say it. Eventually, by saying it often, the awkwardness changes and love becomes very easy and enjoyable to express. When parents understand that we love them for what they "ARE," they tend to become more loving and accepting of us.

Just as important as telling our parents that we love them is the physical expression of love. (Positive body language) Kissing parents hello, holding them (hugging), and just touching their hand with ours are all very significant ways to show the rents how we feel about them. *You might be surprised how well they respond to this, as well as how much you enjoy it too! At the age of twenty-seven, I still kiss my mother and father hello -- even when in public. Try it, you'll like it.*

Eventually, our parents will not only be our parents, but the closest of friends. We will have developed a very special relationship which will lead to a happier family life. Moreover, the world is a mighty big place and "belonging" to our family gives us inner strength.

Please consider this very serious thought: Because each parent is so unique and different, it is my personal belief that it is impossible to feel the same toward both parents, so don't be disappointed if you don't. Believing that we can or should feel the same for each parent can cause unnecessary guilt and bad feelings about ourselves.

Compliments and Flattery Will Get You
Everywhere

If your parents are like mine, they love to be appreciated. Even when the appreciation is bull-paddies, they still love appreciation! After all, **parents are most**

proud and happy when they feel that their child is happy and appreciates and loves them.

In order to truly manage parents, we **MUST** show appreciation for them on a regular basis. **By being appreciative of their efforts and thanking them often, parents are much more apt to do more things for us.** *We are in reality, training them to do what we want!*

Whenever my parents do anything for me, I thank them. *They just eat it up with a spoon! A simple, "Thank you," is so quick, easy, painless, and very inexpensive that we would have to be nimrods if we didn't take advantage of saying it.*

Whenever our parents have done something for us such as, taking us on a vacation, dropping us off at a friend's house, buying us some gizmo that we really wanted or just saying something nice to us, thank them. It is also very important that we explain to our parents why we liked what they did since this helps them to understand what we like.

The best possible place to thank or compliment a parent is in public, especially around their friends. It shows whoever heard our compliment that we have been "well-raised" and are truly appreciative. *We earn thousands of brownie points with the rents when we compliment them in public.*

Kiss ass! Give compliments to parents for things that you know they work hard for or care a lot about. Say nice things to them so that they feel good. When parents feel good around us, they will have good feelings for us. Remember, parents often become what we tell them they are, so tell them that they are wonderful, generous, nice, generous, kind, generous, caring, loving and of course. . . generous.

If what they say is meaningless, agree with their statement instead of arguing for the sake of arguing. Saying: "I agree with you,""You're absolutely right," "That is a good idea," etc. will make any parent feel great! *Just don't let them know what you are doing!*

Giving gifts to parents is also helpful. Whether it is something that we made especially for them or just a restaurant mint, our actions and good intentions toward them will be appreciated and rewarded!

Respect

Respect is a popular word that parents love to use. Have you ever heard your parents say, "Respect your elders" or from a different point of view, "Don't be disrespectful," or even,"You **must** show respect for your parents."

*Weren't they the boneheads who hinted that respect is always **"EARNED,"** not given?*

Although we may have trouble actually respecting our parents, we **SHOULD** show our parents respect. *Before you call me a double-crosser, keep reading. . .* This is **NOT** to say that we have to agree with:

- what they think
- what they believe
- what they feel
- their ideals
- what they tell us to do
- their own actions
- their personal preferences
- their taste in dress
- their needs and desires

But, to successfully manage our parents, we really must respect our **parents' RIGHT** to:

- think what they want
- believe what they want
- feel what they want
- hold their own ideals
- express themselves as they wish
- act as they see fit
- dress as they wish
- fulfill their needs and desires

Don't we want these same RIGHTS too?

Just as we allow our friends to have these rights, shouldn't we extend them to our parents? If not, how can we expect them to give these rights to us? Respect should be mutual. Besides, showing respect for a person's rights is something that makes that person feel good toward us. It gives them the feeling and satisfaction that we approve of what they "are." This is especially true for our parents.

Best of all, with mutual respect, parents will be more willing to fulfill our needs and desires, as well as listen more closely to our opinions and beliefs.

If you are treated disrespectfully by your parents, ask yourself how you treat them. We, as kids, must realize that respect must start with us. Our parents just are not going to respect our rights first. *It's the nature of the beast, literally!*

Bribery

Bribes are an extremely useful tool. *Stop shaking your head. Don't try to bribe your parents. I know; it's a waste of time.* **Instead, let your parents bribe you!** Let them get accustomed to giving you something when you do something for them. After all, if we are going out of our way for our parents, it is only fair that we get something in return.

It must be stated that if we are not giving anything to our parents in our relationship, and are only taking, we have little leverage with them. Think of rents as a checking account *in more ways than one!* We can only withdraw what we have deposited.

Recently, I witnessed my friend's mother bribe her son to do her a favor. I was astounded by what she

95

bribed him with: an African nail fetish! Being the mental pygmy that I am, I naturally asked her what an African nail fetish was. Her response was, "I really don't know, but it's what he wants." Here was a true master. (And I thought I had my parents trained!)

My friend, laughing hysterically in front of his mother, described what an African nail fetish was. A little despondently, she turned to me and asked, "I've always had to bribe my son to do things. Do your parents have to bribe you too?" I told her, "It's my favorite form of motivation!" Well, it is my favorite form of motivation, and besides, we kids have to stick together.

She was very happy to hear my reply. I guess the saying, "misery loves company" is true. To my buddy. . . I tip my hat!

Bribery should definitely be used when we know that in the end, parents will probably try to force us to do something. By allowing ourself to be bribed, we get something out of the deal, instead of just getting rooked.

Incidentally, if you are wondering what an African nail fetish is, it is my uneducated understanding that an African nail fetish is an animal or human figure that represents a certain deity. When a favor is asked of this deity, a piece of iron is driven into the figure.

Responsibility

Responsibility is one of the greatest torches an adult (especially a parent) carries, *a torch I would like to ram up their butt.* Have you ever heard a parent utter or mutter, "Why can't you be more responsible?" or "Try to be a little more responsible for a change."

What is responsibility and why do adults need us to act in this way?

I believe responsibility is:
- being dependable and reliable
- being honest
- being trustworthy
- being thoughtful and considerate
- accepting blame for something we know we
    have done wrong
- being accountable for our own actions
- following through to complete a task
- being safe and careful
- not getting into trouble *that we can't get
    out of*
- keeping up with our work, chores, school, etc.
- being on time or calling when we are running
    late
- cleaning up after ourselves

The following simple thought best illustrates the tremendous power we can possess by being responsible. **The more responsibility we show, the more trust, freedom, and privileges will be given to us, since we will be deserving.**

To become more "responsible," here are two easy rules to remember:
A. Completely understand what is being asked of you so you can be "responsible" in fulfilling all "responsibilities." (Ask questions if there is any confusion about what is being asked of you.)
B. If you can not do something or know that you won't do something, be honest with your parents and **tell them,** so you won't be irresponsible.

Tricks For Doing Well In School
Don't get frightened by the title of this section,

because school is a piece of cake if you know a couple of tricks. Please hang with me and keep reading.

What are the six best reasons to get good grades in school:

6) Good grades earn you respect by peers, teachers, and parents;

5) Good grades help you to get into a good college and get a good job;

4) Good grades indicate that you are learning and your mind is growing;

3) Good grades help you obtain new privileges and freedoms,

2) Good grades help build your confidence and self esteem;

1) Good grades help you accomplish your goals.

The bottom line is -- by getting good grades, you do well for yourself. As my Mom has always told me, "Ignorance is only bliss if you are ignorant." I do hate quoting my Mom, but she is right in this instance. (It also explains why she is so blissful!)

Although some of the following ideas are common sense and some may be a little devious, here are some ideas for getting good grades which I have used:

1. "The Smoke Screen" The first impression you give anyone is always important, but especially so with teachers. **If you win your teacher over in the first month of class, most of the battle is won for any class you will ever have with that teacher for the rest of your school career!**

To win your teacher over, sit in the front row of class, pay attention, do your work, participate, don't screw around in class, visit with the teacher after class for just a minute to talk, have a positive attitude, and **try your hardest to get an A on the first test or paper.** *Don't worry what your friends will think, for if they are TRUE friends, your attitude in class should be meaningless.*

Getting that A on your first test or paper is of utmost importance, because all teachers use the first grade or two to determine a student's capabilities. Best of all, when a new teacher asks one of your old teachers what kind of student you are, their answer will be a positive one. Teachers do talk/gossip.

2. "Time Wise." Don't put work aside, procrastinate and then do a rushed and sloppy job. Prepare for tests and papers in advance. Just do it and get it over with quickly.

3. "Human Relations." Realize that every teacher is a person with their own problems, aversions, and idiosyncrasies. Get to know what they like in a student and be that type of student, *or at least appear to be that type of student!* If you are trouble in a class, *and we all know what can be characterized as trouble,* your teacher will not like you.

Do everything possible to make the teacher feel great about you so that when they are correcting your test or paper and see that it is yours, they may only take off three points instead of five points. After all, they are the teacher and can grade a paper or test any way they choose (especially on essay questions which are subjective).

The contrary is also true. Never do things that annoy or anger a teacher, *and we all know what they are!* If this happens, they will dislike giving you a good grade, even if you deserve one. *Don't be so naive as to think that a teacher does not look to see whose paper or test they are grading before they begin to grade it.*

4. "Friendliness." Be friendly to all teachers, and always say "hello" when you walk in the room and "good bye" and "thank you" when the class is over. Genuinely compliment them whenever possible, *even though with some teachers this may be very difficult!* Compliments

Yeah, Yeah, put it in the pile with your other ones, you little brown-noser....!

are easy, take little time and effort, and reap incredible rewards.

The bottom line is -- when teachers like you and are **FRIENDS,** they will do everything within their power to help you.

5. "Money." Get your money's worth by asking questions during or after class. *Don't be afraid to ask questions!* Furthermore, there is absolutely nothing wrong with going to teachers for extra help, since that is

what they are paid to do. *If you are too proud, get help from a fellow classmate who does well in your class. In doing this, you will also be making a friend.*

A wonderful ploy which I used in class was asking a question on a subject to which I already knew the answer. Then, I would interrupt and solve my own question before the teacher could finish explaining her answer. It didn't stop there; I would then thank the teacher for helping me and this would make them feel valuable (how wrong they were!). I know it's corny, but it works!

Another technique that I used to show a teacher that I cared for their "beloved subject," was to go after class and ask them to go over some specific question(s) that I had missed on the last test. Even when I did well on a test (the best time to do this), I would ask them to show me my error. This showed the teacher that I was conscientious, caring, and ambitious. In fact, on a couple of occasions, I would get some credit back on the test when I sold them on the idea that I had only made a partial mistake!

6. "HELP!" Ask your parents to help you with your homework, *unless they are meatheads! For example, I would never ever ask my Mom to help me with math since I would have flunked the test.* (When parents help, they get to spend time with us in a positive way and also see first hand that we are "responsible students".)

7. "Bribery." A great motivator to improve grades is an agreement with parents where money is rewarded for good grades. *Bribery. I love bribery! For me, it worked like this: for an A, I received $5.00, a B was worth $3.00, and a C was not worth any money. If I made a D or an F, I paid $3.00 or $10.00 respectively.*

8. "Common Sense." Try your hardest to do well. The feeling of success and accomplishment will drive you to even higher achievements.

Precedents

Precedents are examples, acts, or past decisions upon which someone bases future decisions. Precedents are great tools for managing parents since parents themselves set the precedents. They are especially useful if you have an older sibling who has broken ground for you.

Here is an example of how I used precedents: *My sister was allowed to get her driver's license when she was fifteen. Once my parents did this, it was assumed that when I was fifteen, I could also get my driver's license.*

Warning: Be careful how precedents are used, because they can backfire and be used against us. Parents can use precedents set by our older siblings to attempt to control us. For example: *When I was fourteen and a half, I tried to convince my parents to give me my learner's permit, but was unsuccessful since my sister had not been allowed to get hers.*

If you don't have an older sibling, there are no pre-established precedents, so you must start from scratch. Remember, don't be afraid to ask for anything, because everything is negotiable. It is only the price that needs to be established. *Go get 'em.*

Multiple Choice:

Managing parents is:
  A. Not important.
  B. Ignoring their needs.
  C. Using a cattle prod to get what we want.
  D. Influencing their values in different ways to get
     what we desire.

Whenever possible, tell your parents:
  A. How much they mean to you.
  B. How much you care about them
  C. How much you appreciate everything they do for
     you.
  D. How much you love them and show your love by
     kissing, touching or holding them.
  E. All of the above.

Your dad has just finished cleaning all of the windows:
  A. Ignore him.
  B. Tell him he has been doing it wrong.
  C. Tell him he has done a very sloppy job and should
     be ashamed of himself.
  D. Compliment his work and if he is really finished
     and there is nothing else left to do, be gra-
     cious and offer to help.

When you want your mother to buy you a walkman, say
  A. "Buy me that walkman."
  B. "Buy me that walkman NOW, or else!"
  C. "Buy me that walkman now, or I'll set the house on
     fire."
  D. "I would really appreciate it if you would please
     buy me that walkman."

Your mom just bought a new dress and asks you what you think. To flatter her and make her feel good about you, answer her:
A. It makes you look a little overweight.
B. It makes you look a little like a blimp.
C. If you had an apple in your mouth, you would look like a baked pig.
D. It would look better on someone else. You know, someone attractive.
E. It's a really pretty dress and makes you look super.

Your mom, all dressed up, has just walked into your room. She is smiling and has not said a word. You should tell her:
A. What do you want?
B. Why can't you ever leave me alone?
C. What have I done wrong now?
D. Would you please leave me alone?
E. Cowabonga! Your outfit looks great! Where are you going?

Your father is very proud of the work he has done to improve the house. You should tell him:
A. It's about time you got that work done!
B. That's a sloppy job. Do it over.
C. That's a pretty good job, considering you did it.
D. Wow! That's a great job. You must be proud of your work.

You want your mom and dad to feel good about you. Tell them:
A. You are terrific.
B. You are really wonderful.
C. I really appreciate all the caring and love you give to me.
D. You do so much for me. Can I do anything for you?
E. I love you.
F. All of the above.

Your mom or dad just did a favor for you. You should
say:
- A. Thank you very much. I really appreciate the
     favor.
- B. Thank you very much. I really appreciate the
     favor.
- C. Thank you very much. I really appreciate the
     favor.
- D. All of the above.

The following are reasons why we should be
"responsible":
- A. Because it shows that we are trustworthy.
- B. Because it makes our parents feel good about us.
- C. Because it makes our parents happy.
- D. Because it will help us to gain more freedom and
     privileges.
- E. All of the above and especially D!

If we act "responsibly," parents will:
- A. Show us more trust.
- B. Give us more privileges.
- C. Feel better toward us.
- D. Give us more freedom.
- E. All of the above.

We should respect:
- A. The American Flag.
- B. Apple pie.
- C. Rock n' Roll.
- D. Our parents' RIGHTS.
- E. All of the above.

In order to do well in school, we need to:
A. Neglect doing all of the work required of us.
B. Daydream in class about the classmate that we are in love with.
C. Ignore what is being taught.
D. Cheat.
E. Work smart, work hard, and try our best.

If we want to do well in a particular class, we should:
A. Pass notes to get the teacher pissed off at us.
B. Talk when the teacher talks and interrupt them.
C. Read the latest magazine by putting it inside of our note book.
D. Put chalk in the erasers to aggravate the teacher.
E. Get our teacher to like us as a friend by being a friend, by being considerate of them, and by respecting their desire to teach.

Doing well in school will:
A. Increase your knowledge and understanding of the world.
B. Will give you a feeling of self-respect and achievement.
C. Help you to get into college.
D. Stop parents from bitching and complaining about your grades.
E. Reap rewards and privileges from your parents.
F. All of the above.

Chapter 10: How <u>NOT</u> To Manage Parents

As stated earlier, negative motivators make our parents do things for us for the wrong reasons.

To manage parents, read the following very carefully! **I do NOT believe in using negative motivation on anyone, especially parents. It can cause pain, hurt feelings, and damage a relationship. If you use any of the following to get what you want from your parents, you should think about changing your management techniques. Negative actions incur negative feelings and the costs definitely outweigh the potential benefits.**

Negative Motivator: Threats

I do not believe in threats. A threat, as defined by <u>Webster's Dictionary</u>, is "an expression of an intention to inflict pain, injury, evil, or punishment on a person or thing." *I like this definition because it precisely explains how cold and evil a threat really is.* **Threats are one of the most destructive motivators that you can use to manage anyone, much less parents. DO NOT USE THEM!** By making a threat, you may be forced to hurt someone, or possibly even yourself!

When I was much younger and even more immature than I am now (it is hard to believe that this is possible), I would make bogus threats like, "If you don't let me. . . , I'll pull my hair (or something to this effect)." When my parents said no, I realized that the clump of hair that I held in my hand was a painful price, as well as a good lesson in stupidity. They probably just viewed my action as saving them a trip to the barber.

It is my feeling that we should never threaten anyone, especially our parents. We lose in many ways:

1) We hurt our parents for we have threatened them and they love us.
2) Our parents will probably lose respect for us, some thing we have worked so hard to build.
3) We may actually have to carry out our threat with the possibility of hurting ourselves or someone else.

Here is an earthshaking threat we all make to our parents that is a monumental mistake: "I don't care." This simple statement is a terrible threat if you really do care. In trying to threaten or shake up a parent, it only gives them an open door to do whatever they want. In saying this, we have tried to manipulate our parents and have instead maneuvered ourselves into a corner!

Negative Motivator: Taking Parents On A Guilt Trip

Most parents feel guilt for one thing or another. Whether it is something that they did or something that they did not do, they have guilt. Using guilt is bad because it is painful and it can backfire! *Since I hate when parents try to use guilt on me, I don't use it on them, except in a **playful way**.*

For example: *Some kid on T.V. mentioned how fantastic the 64 crayon-set with the built-in sharpener was. I quickly looked at my mom and told her how much more wonderful my youth would have been if I had had this set or at least a crayon set with a gold and silver crayon in it when I was in kindergarten. We had a great time battling over the importance of colored wax and really enjoyed ourselves.*

Negative Motivator: Blackmail

If you have information about a parent that they don't want distributed to anyone else, you are in a position to blackmail them.

Never use blackmail because the person you blackmail will eventually get even, and rightly so. Furthermore, the person being blackmailed will lose trust in you.

I once made this mistake with my Mom. Here is what happened: Every month when Mom tries to balance her checkbook, she rarely succeeds. Dad has to come to her rescue, but in the process, he gives her a tough time. I found it very funny hearing him ask her questions like, "How can you write two checks with the same number?" or "Why can't you add and subtract correctly?"

On one occasion when my Mom was struggling with

*her checkbook, I suggested that she do a favor for me or I would tell Dad about her typical book keeping mess. She told me, "I wouldn't do that," but I pushed further. Realizing that I was serious, she told me that she would never be blackmailed. **SHE** then called my father into the room and told him everything. This definitely was not part of my plan! At this point, all I could do was try to dodge accusations and threats from both of the rents.*

I learned a valuable lesson that day in that I would never try to blackmail anyone and would never allow myself to be blackmailed.

Negative Motivator: Begging

Where begging is concerned, unless you are in a situation in which your life is in danger or you could get hurt, don't beg. *Where our parents are concerned, never beg. Have some self-esteem! Some self-respect! Don't be a spineless jelly fish and grovel to anyone, much less your rents. Instead, try to make them grovel to you!*

In all seriousness, begging and its extreme, whining, are terrible managerial tools that create pity for us. *Begging and*

whining are like the constant crying of a baby, quite tire-some. When someone does something for us out of pity, in the process they lose a lot of respect for us. What an expensive price to pay!

Negative Motivator: Not Caring For Our Parents

Life is a big circle and you will find that your relationship with your parents will change dramatically as everyone gets older. When born, we are totally helpless and our parents take care of us. As we and our parents get older, we may become responsible for our parents.

Making negative comments regarding how we will or will not care for our parents is BAD!

When my sister and I were young and naive, without knowing better, we occasionally joked in a humorous way of how we would take care of our parents when they got older. They would joke with us too.

We would discuss the type of old folks home in which they would live and how often we would visit them. Then, we would change our minds, feeling that the cost of an old folks home is too high. Finally, we would discuss the pros and cons of Eskimo health care for the elderly, the myth of putting the elderly on an ice-flow and waving good-bye.

While all these comments were in jest, I now realize that it most probably was painful for them. Discussing death with parents in this way is cold and I'm very sorry we did it.

If you too, have found thinking about death painful, we share the same feeling. Reality, however, forces us to realize that we should not go around thinking that we will live forever. If we do, we might put off important things until later and then have regrets when we run out of time.

    The following poem delicately expresses these feelings:

> Birth is a beginning
> And death a destination,
> And life is a journey:
> From childhood to maturity
> And youth to age;
> From innocence to awareness
> And ignorance to knowing;
> From foolishness to discretion
> And then, perhaps, to wisdom;
> From weakness to strength
> Or strength to weakness-
> And, often, back again;
> From health to sickness
> And back, we pray, to health again;
> From offense to forgiveness,
> From loneliness to love,
> From joy to gratitude,
> From pain to compassion,
> And grief to understanding-
> From fear to faith;
> From defeat to defeat to defeat-
> Until, looking backward or ahead,
> We see that victory lies
> Not at some high place along the way,
> But in having made the journey, stage by stage,
> A sacred pilgrimage.
> Birth is a beginning
> And death a destination.
> And life is a journey,
> A sacred pilgrimage-
> To life everlasting.
>   -ANONYMOUS

Time is very dear and once it's gone, it's gone forever.
We should use it wisely.

Multiple choice:

In managing our rents, some tactics we should we should **NOT** use are:
  A. Blackmail.
  B. Threats.
  C. Begging.
  D. All of the above.

Chapter 11: Combatting Parental Tricks

As important as it is to know the different tools available to manage our parents, it is also important to understand the different techniques that parents use to manage us (or should I say manipulate us)! Because parents have controlled our lives in the past, they feel that they can dictate terms which we must blindly follow. They are wrong! Keep this in mind when dealing with them, because you really do have some say.

Threats and Intimidation

Threats and intimidation (intimidation is when someone tries to make you feel timid or frightened) are forms of control which parents just love to use. They howl and threaten us with all sorts of punishments, *as well as scream, rant, and rage.* At their leisure, they can act like total dictators *or more appropriately stated, lunatics!*

When anyone, especially a parent, uses intimida-

tion, they are either on the defensive or are too lazy to use diplomacy.

Whatever the reason for using intimidation or threats, all you really need to know is how to handle the situation when it arises.

Here is what to do: Without interrupting them, talk in a firm, but understanding voice and try to make them re-evaluate the situation as to whether or not a threat or a loud voice is truly merited. By not showing fear or immediate compliance with their tantrum, you will let them know that their "scare tactic" is not working. This must be done in a respectful way so that they do not lose face.

1. Ask a question like, "Are you trying to frighten/intimidate me?" or "I know that you are angry and frustrated, but is screaming going to help?" When they stop to think of a response, volunteer your side of the story in a truthful manner.

2. Express, through an "I" message, that they are frightening you, such as, "I feel frightened when I am screamed at."

3. Change the subject by telling them that they are acting like one of their own parents. (Where do you think they probably learned to act this way?) This statement should make your mother/father reconsider their actions, because they will reflect on whether or not they liked the way they were once treated, *and will hopefully treat you differently.*

4. "The siege" is waiting out their tantrum using Active Listening. (Such as, "I understand that you are upset about. . . .")

Again, after waiting for them to finish speaking/*screaming*, use active listening and "I" messages. Eventually they will get tired and try to end the conversation, *or more likely, will get bored from hearing*

115

their own voices. At this point, state your own case.

5. When your parents are screaming at you, tell them, "I'm sorry, but I couldn't hear you, could you speak up a little." *Well, this is more than a little sarcastic,* but if they are screaming for no apparent reason, **and** you have a good relationship with your parents, give it a try. They may actually try to scream louder, but this being impossible and probably painful, they will be forced to reduce their voices to more normal, *obnoxious levels.* Even when they do catch the sarcasm in your statement, if they attack your comment, it will be done in a more civil tone.

Be careful, since this technique can really backfire if your parents are in a truly foul mood!

No matter what the reason our parents have for screaming, **just don't let them intimidate you.**

Think For Yourself

I think this section may be one of the most important areas of this book, so please consider the following carefully.

Parents and many adults often want blind obedience from us kids. Blind obedience is for dogs, cats, and other non-reasoning animals, not parents or us kids. **Think for yourself!**

Listen to your feelings and decide what is best for you **in all situations.** Adults can intentionally mislead and even outright **lie** to children to get them to do things that are wrong. Kids who blindly obey these adults can become abused or assaulted (physically/sexually, emotionally, or in other ways).

Yes, parents/adults can be mentally screwed up and thereby do emotional or physical harm to their own children or other's children. **If this were to happen to**

you, do not hesitate to go to your parents, school teacher, school counselor/head master, a clergyman, your doctor, another relative, or even a policeman (or all of them) for help. You do have rights so don't be afraid to use them!

Needless to say, try to evaluate the motives behind another person's actions so that you can avoid potential dangers. Listen to your inner feelings. If anyone, including a total stranger, a friend's parent, or even a relative makes you uncomfortable for any reason, do not be afraid to react by screaming "NO" and then running away to get help. Believe in your instincts; the feeling of flight (running away) is a very natural instinct for survival. I must repeat -- you must not be afraid to act by running or screaming for help! It may save your life!

Defend yourself! You are protected under the law (probably even more protected than adults). Do not hesitate to take advantage of these laws by using them. **Worst of all, if you are being abused by another person in any way, do not think that the problem will go away by itself. YOU have to ACT! Just pick up the telephone and dial 911 or 0 (operator) and ask for the police. Tell them your problem. It's that simple.**

The "Talking Back To Parents" Ploy

One of the most frustrating and successful tactics a parent can use to shut us up is to accuse us of "back talking." For example, they say: "Don't back talk me," "Don't talk back to me," or "Don't sass me." Now, any expression of your thoughts is considered: back talk, talking back, or sassing. *Parents sure are tricky!*

The best way to counter this type of attack is to **ask them a question** such as: "Okay, I'm sorry, can I defend myself?" or "Am I entitled to voice an opinion?" If they say yes, then state your position. If they say no, *(trade your parents for a future draft pick)* ask why not. Attack their fallacious statement with your own question or series of questions about your "rights," and you will get around their trickery. *Eventually, this tomfoolery of theirs will become useless, and they will stop using it.*

Guilt Trips

Yes, parents use guilt trips too. Have you ever heard a parent say something like, "I do so much for you and ask for so little. . ." or "After all I have done for you, how can you. . ." or "You don't care about me." *The list goes on and on as you probably know.*

Parents should not control us in this manner, so do not let them.

The best response on your part is to:

1. Confront your parent. Without mincing your words, tell them that they are trying to make you feel

guilty and that you do not appreciate it.

2. Use questions such as, "Are you trying to make me feel guilty?" This directly attacks their statement, for they can't answer "yes" without giving away their true intentions. When they say no, tell them, "Then I won't feel guilty" and you are off the hook.

The more you give in to a parent's use of guilt, the more they will use guilt on you. You must wean them from this habit as soon as possible. Parents must learn that guilt is useless and that "constructive" methods of management will work better.

Comparisons

It amazes me how cruel our parents can be when they compare us to our brother(s) and/or sister(s). *Personally, I feel jealous toward my sister and anger toward my parents when they discuss my shortcomings in such a cold way.*

Do not let your parents get away with this type of foul management and do not stoop to their level by trying to compare them to someone else. Just use "I" messages and questions such as, "I feel jealous of (your brother/sister) when I am compared to them. Is this what you want me to feel?"

Multiple Choice:

Your mother is screaming at you. You should:
A. Tell her that she looks great when her face is beet red.
B. Scream back at her.
C. Wilt like a flower in the wind.
D. Don't be intimidated. Use "Active Listening" and "I" Messages to try to overcome her tantrum. (For example: "Mom, you are angry with me for. . . I feel I did nothing wrong because. . .")

Your dad has just said, "Don't talk back to your elders, you must respect them." You should respond to his statement by:
A. Keeping to yourself and following his B.S.
B. Telling him that not all elders deserve respect.
C. Laughing in his face.
D. Telling him that the days of blind respect are over.
E. Telling him, "May I defend myself or state my opinion?"

The parent of a friend suggests that you do something that makes you feel very uncomfortable. You should:
A. Never blindly obey anyone and listen to your inner feelings because there might be some danger to you.
B. Get more information by questioning your friend's parent as to why they want you to do what they want.
C. Call your own parent, close relative, or friend of the family whom you trust and ask their opinion.
D. Take a taxi home.
E. Any and All of the above.

A stranger has confronted you on the street.
A. Do NOT stop to listen. Run and/or scream, "NO" and seek help and safety quickly.

A close relative of the family has touched your body in an intimate way. You feel upset, uncomfortable, and/or confused. You should:
A. Talk to a parent about exactly what happened, leaving nothing out.
B. Talk to a clergyman or school counselor and tell them exactly what happened, leaving nothing out.
C. Call your doctor on the phone and tell him/her exactly what happened, leaving nothing out.
D. Call the police by dialing 911 or "0" for operator (as soon as an operator answers, ask for the police). When a police officer answers, tell the police officer exactly what happened, leaving nothing out.
E. Any and/or All of the above.

Chapter 12: More Tools, Techniques, and Tips
To Manage Parents

Getting Privacy From Parents

The best way to keep parents out of our room is not to give them an excuse to enter in the first place! This means keeping it clean and orderly so that they have absolutely no reason to go into it and clean up *and snoop around through our stuff*. If possible, negotiate an agreement that as long as you keep your room neat and orderly, they will stay out and leave your "stuff" alone.

YES SON, AS A MATTER OF FACT, I DO DUST THE INSIDES of DRESSER DRAWERS... WHAT ARE YOU DOING HOME SO SOON ??!

If you do not want your parents to find something personal, hide it where they will not find it. In other words, do not hide anything under your bed or mattress, or in a drawer or closet. Hide your more personal items in areas of the house that do not get much traffic or tape them under a shelf or piece of furniture. The best rule for hiding anything is: "where there is dust, there is privacy."

Get Along With Your Parents

You and I both know what gets under our parents' skins, what really irritates the hell out of them and makes them "flip out!" For some reason, we often feel proud of having this ability. If you are grinning, you should be ashamed!

Aggravating our parents for our own kicks and amusement, or to get even should be **stopped!** It is incredibly painful to our parents as well as destructive to our relationship.

Just as we should avoid trying to anger them, we should also avoid arguing with them just for the sake of proving ourselves right, *or, more realistically, proving them wrong.* **Most importantly, this is the type of battle that we should intentionally lose so they will give into us later.** Do yourself a favor. When you feel a senseless fight is about to happen, take command of the situation and prevent it from happening!

Dealing With Confusion and Frustration

When we feel utterly confused or frustrated with our parents, or anyone else for that matter, I believe it is either due to our NOT understanding:

    1) Our own feelings and thoughts; or

    2) Our parents' feelings, thoughts, or actions.

Solving this confusion is easy since it is simply taking the time and effort to explore our own thoughts/feelings or discussing with our parents, their thoughts, feelings, or actions.

This brings to mind that when a **parent** is frustrat-

123

ed with **us,** we should take the time to "de-frustrate" them by simply sharing with them our feelings and thoughts. By letting them know "WHY" we are behaving the way we are, we can alleviate much of their confusion, *or at least reduce their confusion to more normal levels.*

Don't Always Do The Expected

Parents use past experiences to determine why we act the way we do and what our true motives are. When we behave extra nice and with understanding, a parent's immediate reaction is, "What do you want?"

A way we can have fun with a parent (without getting in trouble), is by acting super nice and understanding for no apparent reason. Try it. When your father gets home from work, ask him all sorts of questions like, "What can I do for you?" "Do you want anything from the kitchen?" Compliment him on the way he looks. Ask how he is feeling or how his day was at the office.

Eventually, he will stop and ask you, "What do you want?" Start grinning like the cat that got the canary and simply tell him, "nothing." *He'll probably be confused for the rest of the night!*

Looking For "The Hidden Message"

If a parent does or says something that just does not make sense or is totally wacky, evaluate whether there is a hidden problem, feeling, or concern outside of the conversation that is affecting their actions. If you can determine what that outside force is, you may be able to find the problem and solve it.

For example, every time you go out with your friend who has a jeep, your mom goes bezerk! "The Hidden Message" is that your mom's brother was killed one night when his jeep flipped over. If you didn't know about her fear of jeeps, you probably would feel very frustrated or angry about her seemingly unreasonable reactions. When you finally discover the source of her feelings toward jeeps, you can reassure her that you will use sound judgement by driving carefully or by using another car.

Use Your Age

When parents forget that we are inexperienced *and that we are not brain surgeons,* they can become over demanding or unreasonable with their expectations. The best way to bring them down to earth is to remind them of our age by saying something like, "Hey! I'm just a kid" or "Aren't you expecting a little too much from someone my age?"

When You have Done Something Wrong

When you have done something wrong **and have a pretty good feeling that your parent(s) WILL find out,** here is how to handle them:

1) **YOU** confront them with the truth about what you have done wrong. In doing this, you get to pick the time and place for them to find out, and they get to hear your version of the story first. *Do not lie or pretend to be innocent, because this just infuriates parents more, meaning even bigger trouble!*

2) Show them that you are genuinely sorry and that it won't happen again, by saying something like, "I'm really sorry. **It won't happen again.**" *Easy enough and finally. . .*

3) Do not ask for mercy. Admit that you were wrong and suggest some punishment that you hope will be a fair remedy. *Of course, a lenient punishment should be suggested unless you have really screwed up!* For example, if you have broken a window, suggest that you

will call a repairman to get it fixed and offer them a buck or two toward its repair.

These three actions (especially the second) are all a parent will ask for anyway. By voluntarily sharing the truth, your punishment will probably be less severe than had you not said anything at all.

I will never forget the summer before third grade. One morning, the door bell rang and some popular school mates asked me to come out and play with them. I jumped at the opportunity. How could I pass up playing with guys who were so popular?

When we got outside, they told me that they were egging parked cars, and if I got some eggs from my house, I could partake in the great fun. Sneaking back into the house, I got two eggs. On my return, they showed me a parked car that they had egged.

Thinking that this was nothing and that I was really going to impress them, I started bragging that I was going to egg a moving car with its windows rolled down.

Well, the car I was waiting for finally came down the street. With the egg carefully cradled in my right hand, I judged the car's speed and direction, wound up and let the egg fly. As it left my hand, I realized the egg was going to hit its mark, the back seat of the car! The car stopped with a screech! My tremendous feelings of happiness, excitement, and confidence quickly turned into pure fear. I ran!

Hiding behind two trash cans in a dead end near my house, I knew I was in TROUBLE! My heart was beating like a drum and catching my breath was impossible. The next person I saw was my mother and to say she had a stick the size of a telephone pole up her butt is a serious understatement, and I was the person to blame for its being there! My fear and anxiety turned into pure emotion as I admitted to her that I had thrown the egg and started to cry.

I really don't remember much after admitting my blame, as most of it is a blank. From what I've heard, the people in the car had asked "my friends" who threw the egg. They told them, Copey Pulitzer, where I lived

and where I was hiding. (Or more likely, "He went that away." Actually, with such wonderful friends, I'm surprised they didn't tell them my social security number, my blood type and then offer them my first born.)

The car owner pounded on the front door of our house and demanded to speak to my mother. When my mom came to the door, the driver repeated to my mother what "my friends" had told her. As my Mom tells the story, she couldn't believe what she was hearing and kept denying the possibility that her "perfect" son had thrown an egg into anyone's car. (Well, it was a "perfect" throw!)

127

Finally, Mom realized that I was nowhere to be found and, finding this mighty peculiar, decided to find me.

Punishment. You are probably asking how I was punished. Which device in their well stocked torture chamber was used? Fortunately, all I had to do was live with regret and pay for the cleaning of the inside of the car. That was all. Mom tells me that since I had been so truthful and had taken the whole situation so badly, she was sure I would never do anything similar again.

I sure learned a lot from this painful experience. If you confess the crime, the punishment won't be too severe. I also learned the importance of picking friends carefully and not caving into peer pressure. Finally, when you do something stupid, you will pay for it.

Know When To Cut Your Losses

Sometimes when dealing with parents, they get out of control. *Know what I mean?!? It's as if something crawled up their leg and bit them on their petunia.* This is usually the result of their being in a very emotional state. No matter what you say, they just won't listen and they keep ranting and raging like lunatics! Furthermore, every time you open your mouth, you dig a deeper hole for yourself and get into even more trouble.

When this happens, accept their punishment with no rebuttal and just get away from them. Cut your losses, because there are just times when no method of management will work!

The summer before my freshman year in high school, my friends and I joined a local club where we would go to meet. One evening, a group of us, three guys and two girls, decided we would walk to the local convenience store to buy some alcohol, and if not successful, we would buy some Icees (a New Orleans snowball).

128

Of course everyone got carded, so after purchasing our Icees, we started walking back to the club. Turning the corner, we noticed three guys following us. Just as we began to cross the street, they started running toward us.

Needless to say, someone screamed "RUN!!" and like a herd of frightened antelope with three tigers chasing, we tried to run like the wind! Unfortunately, we only ran like a gentle breeze and they caught up to us.

I was punched once and another guy got hit a couple of times. Finally, we got away from them and headed for a lit house. Never have I run so fast. I couldn't believe it when one of the girls passed me by --and I was trucking!

Pounding on the door of the house, we were let in and we called the police. After the police arrived and we reported what happened, they dropped us off at the club. There, I called my parents to let them know what had occurred.

When finally dropped home, I opened the door and

found my understanding, sympathetic, and caring parents waiting for me. The first words out of my mother's mouth were, "You're punished, go to your room!" Wow, mugged twice in one evening, maybe a world record. Can you believe that when I asked why they were punishing me, they told me that I was being punished for getting mugged when I wasn't supposed to. (I guess when my friends asked me, "Hey Copey, we're going to the Timesaver and then going to get mugged--want to come?" I should have said, "No."

I went to my room. What could I tell them? How can you defend yourself or negotiate with illogic like this?

Later, after my Mom had chilled out, she came in my room and told me I was no longer punished and apologized by explaining that she had just been very upset.

Multiple Choice:

To keep your rents from snooping through your things and out of your room:
  A. Put a sign on your door saying, "Posted: NO TRESPASSING."
  B. Install a burglar alarm on your door.
  C. Hire a doberman watch dog.
  D. Keep your room clean so they have no reason to enter.

When you have done something wrong:
  A. Deny the whole incident.
  B. Blame it on your brother/sister, aunt/uncle, dog/cat and/or the next door neighbor.
  C. Plead temporary insanity.
  D. Confront your parents with the truth, apologize profusely and then suggest a way to remedy the situation.

130

Your mom has just come home from work and you haven't done any of your chores around the house. You should:
  A. Tell her that you had a really tough day at school and to lay off.
  B. Tell her that if she wants it done, she should do the work herself.
  C. Tell her that you don't care what she wants because you are on strike.
  D. Giving no excuse, apologize and tell her that you will get to work right away to take care of the problem. Then, *to stop her mumbling,* tell her that it won't happen again.

Your father seems cross. You then realize that you didn't cut the grass and he had to do **your** chore. You should:
  A. Tell him how much fun you had instead of cutting the grass.
  B. Tell him that although you really hate giving him compliments, he really looks better cutting the grass than you do.
  C. Tell him that it is good that he cut the grass, for it helps to build character and he needs all the help he can get.
  D. Tell him that you hope he cleaned off the mower when he finished, because otherwise it may rust.
  E. Tell him, "You must feel angry with me for forgetting to cut the grass. I'm sorry, it won't happen again."

When your parent are really emotionally upset and on your case, you should:
  A. Tell them to lighten up.
  B. Tell them to take their "beefing" somewhere else.
  C. Tell them to stop busting your chops.
  D. Say nothing and just do whatever you can to get away from them until they cool off.

Conclusion

Well, that's it.

I truly hope this book has helped you to better understand your parents so that you can deal with them more successfully. It can be done!

You may feel that you have so many problems with your parents that you don't know where to start? The answer is to start by picking the easiest and most simple problem you have and apply the ideas and suggestions discussed to solve that problem. Then pick another.

Think of your situation like running a marathon. Twenty-six miles is a long way, but step by step you get closer to the finish line. In fact, after a couple of problems have been solved, you will begin to see that the light at the end of the tunnel is the warm sunlight of success, *not an oncoming train.* Moreover, as you begin to see the finish line, you will be more motivated to run faster!

A significant help in solving our problems occurs when we realize that we are "thinkers" and are willing to make the effort to control our lives. Furthermore, when we realize that the key to working out any problem with our parents is through open and honest communication and by working together, we can have a closer, friendlier, and more loving relationship.

I would like to think that the relationship between a parent and child is based on loving and caring for each other, especially the giving of emotional support at all times. We should spend "quality time" with our parents so that they can get to know us for who we really are: our wants, desires, needs, hopes, aspirations. . . We should also spend time getting to know our parents.

The following poem by Mamie Gene Cole expresses much insight into the relationship between our parents and us.

THE CHILD'S APPEAL

I am the Child.
All the world waits for my coming.
All the earth watches with interest
    to see what I shall become.
Civilization hangs in the balance,
For what I am, the world of tomorrow will be.

I am the Child.
I have come into your world,
    about which I know nothing.
Why I came I know not;
How I came I know not.
I am curious; I am interested.

I am the Child.
You hold in your hand my destiny.
You determine, largely, whether
    I shall succeed or fail.
Give me, I pray you, those things
    that make for happiness.
Train me, I beg you, that I may be
    a blessing to the world.

by **Mamie Gene Cole**

When I have children, I will undoubtedly make poor decisions just as all parents do. Unfortunately, there is no formal school that teaches people how to be good par-

ents, only a person's own childhood and set of values. That's why I'm taking notes now.

Well, it's now up to you. The ideas described are only good if they are used. Try them all. Experiment in the ways you can use them, since some will work better for you than others.

*Never be afraid to dream and see your future. See your dreams and set them as your goals by writing them down on paper. Then determine what changes are necessary and make a plan on how to achieve these goal(s). Although change can be scary and difficult, it is **necessary** (for if you always do what you always do, then you will always get what you always get).*

Remember, think positive, keep smiling and be prepared by anticipating possible opportunities and problems before they happen.

Finally, by working smart, hard and by never quitting, you will turn your dreams into reality and accomplish what you have set out to do. After all, if you want to predict your future, you have to go out and create it.

*Most important of all, believe in yourself, for **YOU CAN MANAGE YOUR PARENTS!***

The End

The following should not be thought of as a legal contract, but an agreement based on **TRUST, HONESTY, INTEGRITY,** and **LOVE.**

On this _____ (date) day of _____ (month), 19____(year), _____ (your parent's name(s)), hereafter known as the "Understanding Party" and_____ (your name), hereafter known as the "Honest Party" agree to the following:

1. OBLIGATIONS OF THE HONEST PARTY (You):
   The Honest Party agrees to:
      A. always speak the TRUTH.
      B. never omit the TRUTH.

2. OBLIGATIONS OF THE UNDERSTANDING PARTY
      (Your Parents):
   The Understanding Party, in recognition and consideration of the Honest Party's honesty and integrity to enter into this agreement and to fulfill the obligations stated under section 1 above, agrees:
      A. not to lose their temper.
      B. to be appreciative toward the Honest Party for telling the TRUTH.
      C. to never cause the Honest Party or anyone else involved, in any way and at any time, to be punished or reprimanded for the Honest Party's fulfillment of the Honest Party's obligations under this agreement.

Agreed to by:

_____ Honest Party

_____ Understanding Party

_____ Understanding Party

The following should not be thought of as a legal contract, but an agreement based on **TRUST, HONESTY, INTEGRITY,** and **LOVE.**

On this _____ (date) day of _____(month) 19___(year), _____(your parents' name(s), hereafter know as the "Understanding Party" and _____(your name), hereafter known as the "Responsible Party," agree to the following:

1. OBLIGATIONS OF THE RESPONSIBLE PARTY (You):
The Responsible Party agrees:

A. that should he or she ever be under the influence of any chemical that impairs his or her ability to function mentally or physically, whether it be alcohol or any other substance, (hereafter known as being "Under the Influence"), he or she will not operate or drive any moving vehicle;

B. never to get into a vehicle with any driver or operator who is Under the Influence;

C. to try to discourage anyone else who is Under the Influence from driving by taking away that person's keys; and

D. that in order to fulfill the above letters A, B, and C, the Responsible Party agrees to call the Understanding Party for a ride home, assistance and/or advice at any time, day or night.

2. OBLIGATIONS OF THE UNDERSTANDING PARTY (Your Parents):
The Understanding Party (your parents), in recognition and consideration of the Responsible Party's honesty and integrity in entering into this agreement to fulfill the obligations stated under section 1 above, agrees:

A. to pick up the Responsible Party, wherever he or she may be, or make arrangements for the Responsible Party's safe transport home;

B. to reimburse the Responsible Party for any and all reasonably incurred expenses in fulfilling his or her obligations to this agreement, including, but not limited to, collect calls and taxi rides home; and

C. **never to cause the Responsible Party or anyone else involved, in any way and at any time, to be punished or reprimanded for his or her being Under the Influence due to the Responsible Party's honesty, integrity and TRUST in the Understanding Party by calling for help.**

Agreed to by:

_____ Responsible Party

_____ Understanding Party

_____ Understanding Party